Eyewitness
TRANSPORTATION

Penny Farthing,
an early bicycle

Pendant in
the shape of a
Phoenician ship

Cutaway
of an internal
combustion engine

Turbofan engine

Lambretta
scooter

Segway
polo
player

Oil tanker

Electric
skateboard

Bell 47
helicopter

Eyewitness
TRANSPORTATION

Written by
LEON GRAY
and
IAN GRAHAM

De Dion Bouton
Model Q

DK Publishing

Indonesian logboat

Insignia of Apollo
missions

LONDON, NEW YORK,
MELBOURNE, MUNICH, AND DELHI

Driving goggles

Consultant Ian Graham

DK DELHI

Project editor Virien Chopra
Project art editor Nishesh Batnagar
Art editor Mahipal Singh
Senior editor Kingshuk Ghoshal
Senior art editor Govind Mittal
Senior DTP designer Tarun Sharma
DTP designer Mohammad Usman
DTP manager Sunil Sharma
Deputy managing editor Eman Chowdhary
Managing art editor Romi Chakraborty
Production manager Pankaj Sharma
Picture researcher Sumedha Chopra
Jacket designer Govind Mittal

DK LONDON

Senior editor Rob Houston
Senior art editor Philip Letsu
US editor Margaret Parrish
Publisher Andrew Macintyre
Production editor Ben Marcus
Production controller Rebecca Short

Brass car horn
in the shape
of a boa

First published in the United States in 2012
by DK Publishing, 375 Hudson Street, New York, New York 10014

Copyright © 2012 Dorling Kindersley Limited

10 9 8 7 6 5 4 3 2 1

001—183293—Jul/12

A catalog record for this book is available
from the Library of Congress.

ISBN 978-0-7566-9062-5 (Hardcover)
978-0-7566-9064-9 (Library binding)

Color reproduction by MDP, UK
Printed and bound by
Toppan Printing Co. (Shenzhen) Ltd., China

www.dk.com

Replica of
Catch-Me-Who-Can, a
locomotive built in 1808

Computer simulation
of a Formula 1 racing car

Soldier of the army of Darius I, from
a frieze in Darius's palace in Iran

Contents

Airbus A380

GOODS TO CUSTOMERS
Since prehistory, goods have been sourced or manufactured in certain places, but need to be transported to market, where customers want to buy and use them. Goods transport, or freight, was developed to get the goods to market. Pack animals, including mules, camels, and yaks, provided the muscle power at first. Long-distance trade routes have existed since the Stone Age, but today, factories are often in different countries than their markets, and trade routes stretch around the globe. Along these trade routes travel cargo ships of all sizes, from river barges to oil tankers. Transporter trucks and freight trains pick up the goods at port and deliver them to their final destination.

Barrier reduces noise pollution

Why travel?

OUR REMOTE, HUNTER–GATHERER ANCESTORS were always on the move, traveling for days on foot in search of food, water, and shelter. When people began to settle as farmers around 8,000 years ago, they began to walk far less to find food. Today, many people go to the store on foot or by car in a trip lasting an hour or less. However, in recent times, people travel more and more as transportation becomes more efficient, faster, cheaper, more comfortable, and accessible to all. They use transportation to travel to school or work, to visit loved ones, to carry goods to market, to tour remote vacation destinations, to explore, or even just to enjoy the journey.

SPREADING ACROSS THE GLOBE
There are many parts of the world that had no humans until people developed sea-going craft and navigation that allowed them to cross oceans. Amazingly, people first arrived in Australia by boat as early as 50,000 BCE, but no one knows what their boats were like. People reached the remote islands of the Pacific much later. They had to travel for weeks without sighting land, so they developed stable canoes with outriggers and sails, such as this modern Hawaiian vessel. They navigated with star charts and by studying wave patterns. These people became known as Polynesians, because between 2,000 and 1,000 years ago, they discovered and settled the hundreds of Pacific islands now called Polynesia.

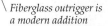
Fiberglass outrigger is a modern addition

LINKING THE WORLD
The Golden Age of Discovery began in the 15th century, when European explorers set sail into the unknown in tall, wooden sailing ships. In the next century, famous explorers, such as Ferdinand Magellan of Portugal and the British captain Francis Drake (pictured) went on royal missions to claim new territories, map the world, and establish trade with remote civilizations. Until these voyages of discovery, people in some parts of the world were completely unaware of each other, and far-flung parts of the known world, such as Europe and China, were rarely in contact. The age of exploration linked the world together, and more people traveled to trade and colonize new lands.

THE DAILY COMMUTE

Every year, the average worker in the US spends more than 100 hours in their daily commute to and from work—the equivalent of nearly three full weeks at work. In the US, 90 percent of people rely on cars to travel to work, creating a buildup of traffic during the morning and evening "rush hours." This rush-hour scene is a busy highway into Atlanta, Georgia. Some people use public transportation such as commuter trains, subways, and trams in an effort to beat the congestion, while others prefer to walk or cycle for shorter journeys.

Vehicle moves slowly due to traffic jam

Many drivers travel alone in their vehicles, increasing congestion and pollution

Pillar supports elevated part of highway

Transporter truck

MILITARY TRANSPORTATION

In ancient times, fighting forces marched on foot or crossed seas in paddle-powered fighting ships. Today, helicopters can take troops directly into a war zone or evacuate them during a speedy retreat. This US Chinook will land in a remote mountain location in Afghanistan, but in some cases, the soldiers drop by parachute. Wars have encouraged developments in transportation technology, such as jet aircraft (see pp. 38–39) during World War II, and spacecraft (see pp. 44–45) during the Cold War.

TRAVELING FOR FUN

Traveling for pleasure is relatively new in the history of transportation. For most people, leisure trips have only become common in the last 100 years. Early vacations were limited to daytrips to the seaside. Trailers and motorhomes meant that people could take comforts with them and gained popularity from the 1930s. Since the 1970s, more people have ventured farther afield on package tours to exotic places. The world seems much smaller than it used to be.

Ford pickup truck

1967 Shasta trailer

THE THRILL OF THE RIDE

Transportation isn't just about getting from A to B—people travel for the sheer thrill of the ride. In ancient times, huge crowds gathered at the Colosseum in Rome to watch fiercely fought chariot races. Today, high-performance racing boats, bikes, cars, and planes provide the spectacle. Here, the Italian Valentino Rossi pops a wheelie before the 2010 San Marino Grand Prix. But the ride doesn't have to be high-powered. The Tour de France bicycle race, now more than 100 years old, is more popular than ever. Sailing boats and hot-air balloons, long impractical compared to motorized craft, still appeal to people who simply enjoy traveling at the mercy of the wind.

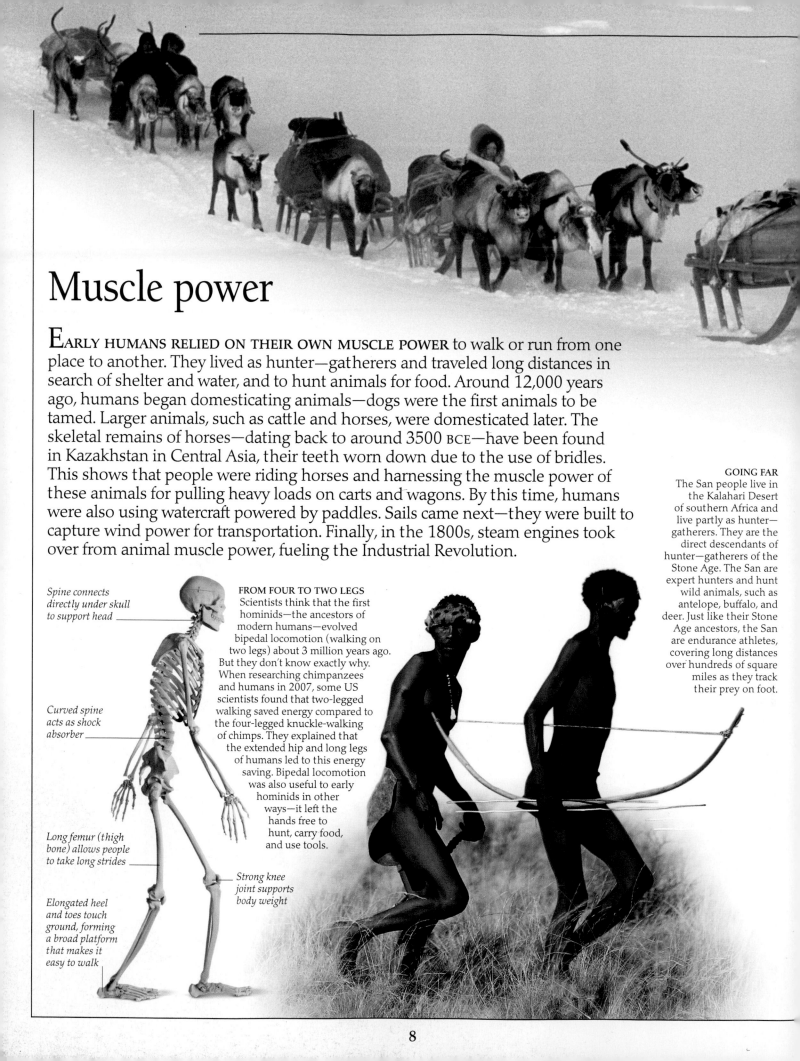

Muscle power

Early humans relied on their own muscle power to walk or run from one place to another. They lived as hunter—gatherers and traveled long distances in search of shelter and water, and to hunt animals for food. Around 12,000 years ago, humans began domesticating animals—dogs were the first animals to be tamed. Larger animals, such as cattle and horses, were domesticated later. The skeletal remains of horses—dating back to around 3500 BCE—have been found in Kazakhstan in Central Asia, their teeth worn down due to the use of bridles. This shows that people were riding horses and harnessing the muscle power of these animals for pulling heavy loads on carts and wagons. By this time, humans were also using watercraft powered by paddles. Sails came next—they were built to capture wind power for transportation. Finally, in the 1800s, steam engines took over from animal muscle power, fueling the Industrial Revolution.

GOING FAR
The San people live in the Kalahari Desert of southern Africa and live partly as hunter—gatherers. They are the direct descendants of hunter—gatherers of the Stone Age. The San are expert hunters and hunt wild animals, such as antelope, buffalo, and deer. Just like their Stone Age ancestors, the San are endurance athletes, covering long distances over hundreds of square miles as they track their prey on foot.

Spine connects directly under skull to support head

Curved spine acts as shock absorber

FROM FOUR TO TWO LEGS
Scientists think that the first hominids—the ancestors of modern humans—evolved bipedal locomotion (walking on two legs) about 3 million years ago. But they don't know exactly why. When researching chimpanzees and humans in 2007, some US scientists found that two-legged walking saved energy compared to the four-legged knuckle-walking of chimps. They explained that the extended hip and long legs of humans led to this energy saving. Bipedal locomotion was also useful to early hominids in other ways—it left the hands free to hunt, carry food, and use tools.

Long femur (thigh bone) allows people to take long strides

Strong knee joint supports body weight

Elongated heel and toes touch ground, forming a broad platform that makes it easy to walk

BEASTS OF BURDEN

Humans domesticated many large animals for use in transportation. Some animals, such as horses, yaks, and camels, were used as "mounts"—people actually rode them. Others were used as "pack" animals to carry goods on their backs or as "draft" animals to pull sleds and carts. Today, some Arctic people use caribou as mounts. Others, such as the Khanty people of Siberia in northern Russia, use caribou as beasts of burden, pulling sleds vast distances in search of food. The ancestors of the Khanty people started to follow caribou herds around 10,000 years ago. They moved with the herd all year, guided by the availability of fresh pasture. Gradually, they domesticated the animal.

HORSE POWER

Archeological evidence suggests that people began to ride horses and use them as draft and pack animals around 4000 BCE in central Asia. By 3000 BCE, the domestication of horses was widespread around Europe and Asia. Riding horses allowed people to travel farther and more quickly than by foot. The armies of many great rulers, such as Philip II of Macedon and his son Alexander the Great, used horses to ride to and conquer faraway lands.

Man riding horse, silver coin from the time of Philip II of Macedon (359–336 BCE)

Pushing pole against riverbed moves raft forward

A woman travels on a bamboo raft on the Li River in China

TRAVELING ON WATER

People invented ways of using muscle power to cross rivers and eventually mastered ways of traveling along rivers and across lakes. The earliest rafts were probably nothing more than floating logs, and people used their hands to steer the rafts on the right course. Eventually, people lashed logs, pieces of tree bark, or reeds together for extra stability. They began to steer rafts using paddles or by pushing long wooden poles against the bottom of the river or lake. The paddle or pole helped channel the muscle power of the navigator.

MARATHON MAN

According to legend, a Greek messenger known as Pheidippides ran for 150 miles (240 km) from Athens to Sparta to ask the Spartans for help in fighting the Persians, who had landed at Marathon. He also ran another 25 miles (40 km) from the battlefield at Marathon to Athens to announce the Greek victory—and then died from exhaustion. The story of his heroic effort inspired the modern running race called the marathon. People continue to test the limits of their endurance by competing in marathons and other long-distance races.

On the water

THE WORLD'S FIRST CIVILIZATIONS grew up near rivers, because these provided water for drinking and for watering crops. At first, rivers may have been a barrier to exploration and expansion, but to people who mastered building and steering water craft, they acted as the first highways. Rafts were already in use in Egypt in 4000 BCE, as shown by pictures on fragments of pottery dated to that time. By this time, some boat builders were carving dugout canoes from tree trunks and others were making boats from animal skins. Eventually, people began using planks of wood to build boats. Initially powered by oars, and later by simple, square sails, wooden boats enabled people to travel longer distances.

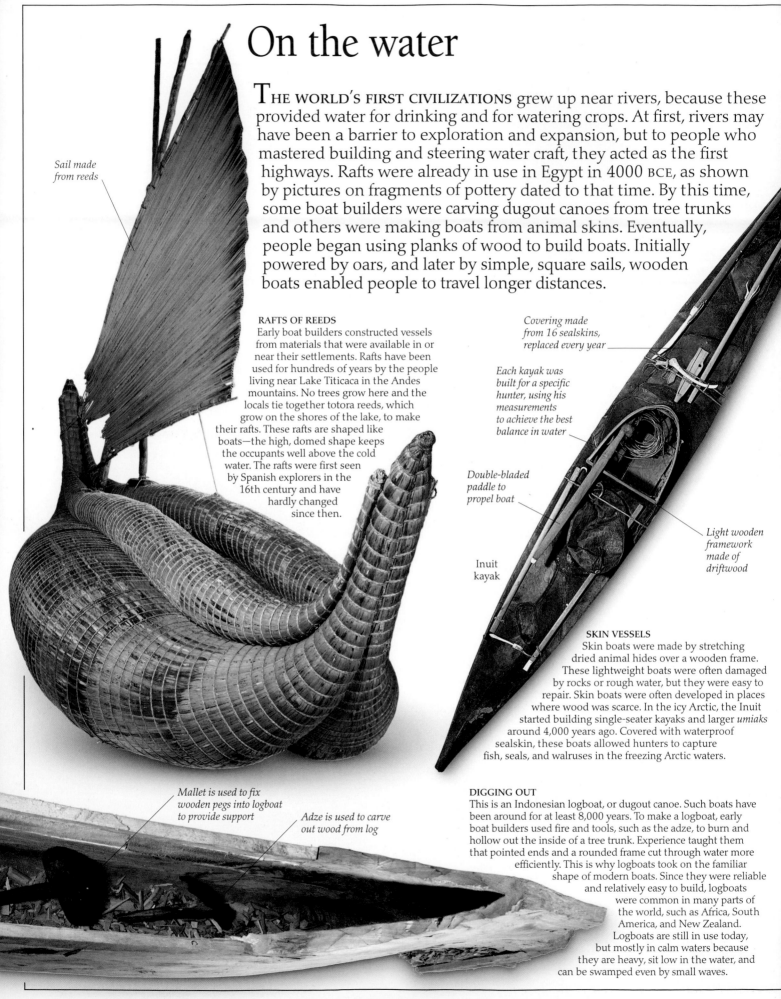

Sail made from reeds

RAFTS OF REEDS
Early boat builders constructed vessels from materials that were available in or near their settlements. Rafts have been used for hundreds of years by the people living near Lake Titicaca in the Andes mountains. No trees grow here and the locals tie together totora reeds, which grow on the shores of the lake, to make their rafts. These rafts are shaped like boats—the high, domed shape keeps the occupants well above the cold water. The rafts were first seen by Spanish explorers in the 16th century and have hardly changed since then.

Covering made from 16 sealskins, replaced every year

Each kayak was built for a specific hunter, using his measurements to achieve the best balance in water

Double-bladed paddle to propel boat

Inuit kayak

Light wooden framework made of driftwood

SKIN VESSELS
Skin boats were made by stretching dried animal hides over a wooden frame. These lightweight boats were often damaged by rocks or rough water, but they were easy to repair. Skin boats were often developed in places where wood was scarce. In the icy Arctic, the Inuit started building single-seater kayaks and larger *umiaks* around 4,000 years ago. Covered with waterproof sealskin, these boats allowed hunters to capture fish, seals, and walruses in the freezing Arctic waters.

Mallet is used to fix wooden pegs into logboat to provide support

Adze is used to carve out wood from log

DIGGING OUT
This is an Indonesian logboat, or dugout canoe. Such boats have been around for at least 8,000 years. To make a logboat, early boat builders used fire and tools, such as the adze, to burn and hollow out the inside of a tree trunk. Experience taught them that pointed ends and a rounded frame cut through water more efficiently. This is why logboats took on the familiar shape of modern boats. Since they were reliable and relatively easy to build, logboats were common in many parts of the world, such as Africa, South America, and New Zealand. Logboats are still in use today, but mostly in calm waters because they are heavy, sit low in the water, and can be swamped even by small waves.

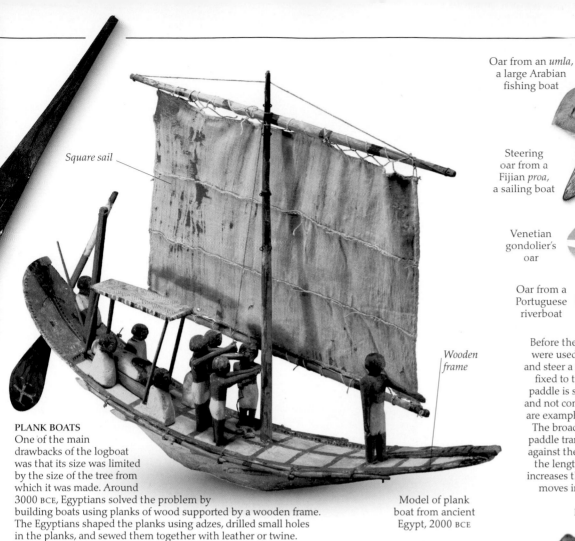

Square sail

Wooden frame

Model of plank boat from ancient Egypt, 2000 BCE

PLANK BOATS

One of the main drawbacks of the logboat was that its size was limited by the size of the tree from which it was made. Around 3000 BCE, Egyptians solved the problem by building boats using planks of wood supported by a wooden frame. The Egyptians shaped the planks using adzes, drilled small holes in the planks, and sewed them together with leather or twine.

Oar from an *umla*, a large Arabian fishing boat

Steering oar from a Fijian *proa*, a sailing boat

Venetian gondolier's oar

Oar from a Portuguese riverboat

Modern-day racing oar

OARS AND PADDLES

Before the invention of sails, oars and paddles were used to propel a boat through the water and steer a steady course. While an oar is usually fixed to the side of the boat by an oarlock, a paddle is supported completely by the paddler and not connected to the boat. Oars and paddles are examples of a simple machine called a lever. The broad, flat blade at the end of an oar or a paddle transmits the pulling force of the rower against the water. This force decreases through the length of the oar or paddle, and, in turn, increases the distance through which the blade moves in water, pushing the boat forward.

MANY PADDLES

Multiple-oared boats were commonly used by Phoenicians from about 1100 BCE. The many rowers gave the vessel a burst of speed. By 700 BCE, extra tiers, or levels, of oarsmen were used to propel boats even faster. These vessels were the *biremes* (two tiers) and *triremes* (three tiers) used by the Greeks and Romans. Multiple-oared and -paddled boats are still in use today, mainly for sports. This boat is being paddled in a race in Kerala, India.

Pendant in the shape of a Phoenician galley, 404 BCE

ANCIENT TRADE

Building bigger boats allowed people to travel longer distances and carry large amounts of cargo. This spurred the growth of trade between distant peoples. The Phoenicians were a seafaring people, who lived from around 1500 to 300 BCE, in the region now known as Lebanon and Syria. Phoenician merchants traded with the Egyptians and Greeks, crossing the Mediterranean Sea in large, oared boats called galleys. We know of such trade because artifacts such as this Phoenician pendant have been found at ancient Greek and Egyptian sites.

THE FIRST WARSHIPS

The ancient Greeks and Romans modified galleys for use as warships. The Romans built towers on the galleys so archers could fire their arrows at an enemy from a greater height. Their vessels were armed with battering rams and catapults to destroy enemy ships. By 100 BCE, the Roman navy was dominating the seas. Around the same time, the role of the galley changed from attack to defense, protecting trade routes and policing coastal waters from pirate attacks.

Coin showing a Roman galley

The wheel

THE IDEA BEHIND THE WHEEL was born in Mesopotamia (present-day Iraq) in around 3500 BCE, when people were spinning clay into different wares using the potter's wheel. At that time, the Mesopotamians were using sleds on runners to drag heavy objects along the ground. Around the same time, an unknown innovator turned two potter's wheels through 90 degrees, placing them on their rims and joining their centers with an axle. This created the first wheels designed for transportation. At first, wheels were heavy solid disks carved from tree trunks. Around 2000 BCE, the Egyptians began to cut out sections of the wheel, strengthening the disk with bars called spokes. This helped them build lighter, faster vehicles.

Wooden peg holds axle in place

Wooden cross piece holds planks together

Tripartite, or three-part, wheel shaped from three wooden planks

Stone being moved

Direction of movement

Log at rear is moved to front to continue rolling surface

ORIGINS OF THE WHEEL
Prehistoric people may have used logs as rollers to move heavy objects over the ground. This could be how the standing stones in Stone Age monuments, such as England's Stonehenge, were transported. According to this idea, teams of men pulled on ropes tied to a stone, and the heavy stone moved over the rolling logs. Workers smeared animal fat over the logs, lubricating them to keep the stone moving. Without knowing it, these early builders were using wheels.

ROLLING DOWN THE AGES
The design of the wheel has changed through the ages, from solid wooden wheels to modern alloy wheels with pneumatic, or air-filled, tires. These changes gradually made wheels lighter and stronger, helping wheeled vehicles to become faster, easier to control, and capable of carrying heavier loads.

Spoke strengthens wheel

Wooden wheel has holes to make it lighter

This wooden wheel has two crescent shapes cut around its center. It dates from around 2000 BCE. It shows the first step in the development of spoked wheels.

The ancient Greeks developed the cross-bar wheel by cutting away even more wood from the disk of the wheel and reinforcing the disk with spokes.

WHEELS OF WAR

Horse-drawn chariots with spoked wheels were first used in funerary processions for Egyptian kings, or pharaohs. Military commanders soon realized that chariots could be put to good use on the battlefield. A fast, light chariot could quickly roll in and attack the enemy. Between 5,000 to 6,000 chariots took part in the Battle of Kadesh, which was fought between the Egyptians and the Hittites in 1274 BCE.

Illustration showing Egyptian pharaoh Ramesses II at the Battle of Kadesh

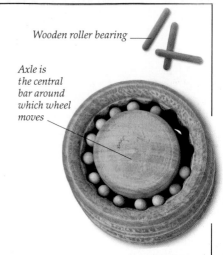

Wooden roller bearing

Axle is the central bar around which wheel moves

A SMOOTH RIDE

In 100 BCE, Danish wagon builders put wooden roller bearings around an axle—the central rod around which a pair of wheels or a wheel turns—and attached it to the chassis, or base, of a vehicle. The bearings rolled between the wheel and the axle, reducing friction and allowing the moving parts to rotate more easily. The vehicle, therefore, required less energy to pull them. This improvement, among others, reduced wear and made rides smoother.

Stone exerts downward force

Metal rim strengthens wheel

Heavy stone, or load

Handle used for pulling vehicle over ground

Direction of movement

Hub keeps wheel firmly joined to axle

Force exerted by weight of stone transfers downward and outward through spokes

Rim of wheel creates inward force that pushes against weight of stone

WHEELS AT WORK

The wheel is a simple machine that overcomes the force of friction by rolling over a surface. The combination of a wheel and an axle is an example of a lever, with the pivot point, or fulcrum, at the center of the axle. As the axle turns around, the rim of the wheel rotates at the same speed, but covers a greater distance. So only a little rotation around the axle results in a lot of forward progress. The weight of the load is spread out through the spokes to the wheel's rim, which is reinforced with metal.

Upward force exerted by ground supports wheel and load

Metal spoke is bolted to central hub to make wheel stronger

Pneumatic rubber tube is filled with air, which helps absorb shocks

Alloy wheel is made from a mixture of metals, such as aluminum and magnesium

Spoked wheels with an iron rim and hub were common from 500 BCE to the beginning of the 20th century. The wheel shown above helped move a heavy Russian cannon.

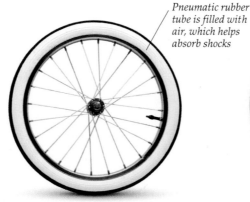

By the late 19th century, bicycle wheels had wire spokes to strengthen the wheel and pneumatic tires to smooth out bumps in the road.

Many modern cars are equipped with wheels made from metal alloys. Alloy wheels are lighter and stronger, but more expensive than the more common steel wheels.

On the road

THE FIRST ROADS DEVELOPED FROM TRACKS formed by the footsteps of countless people and animals following the same routes for millennia. More traffic on the busiest paths made them wider and flatter. These well-used routes, or roads, not only made it easier for people to travel, but also allowed armies to cover vast distances swiftly, enabling rulers to control their empires. Roads also opened up trade routes between far-flung places—the Silk Road and the Amber Road connected regions in Asia with Europe. The advent of wheeled vehicles spurred the development of even better roads, leading to streets paved with bricks and stones.

Ridgeway

WALKING ON HILLS
Ancient tracks called ridgeways followed ridges along the tops of hills. The dry and open ground was easier to navigate than the dense woods lower down in the valleys. The Ridgeway in England is a 85-mile- (137-km-) long track, which travelers, farmers, and soldiers have used for at least 5,000 years. Monuments, tombs, and forts were built near this important route. One such monument is the Uffington White Horse (above)—a mysterious prehistoric hilltop figure made of crushed white chalk. The Ridgeway is the faint hedge line running near the top of this image.

Columns line a paved street, dating to around 39–76 CE, in Jerash, Jordan

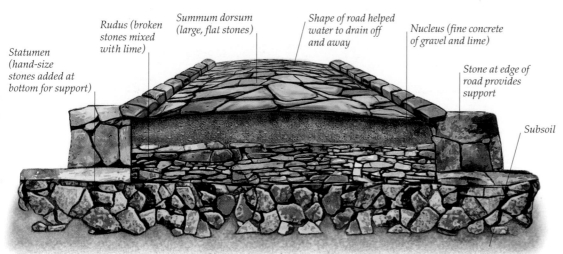

Statumen (hand-size stones added at bottom for support)

Rudus (broken stones mixed with lime)

Summum dorsum (large, flat stones)

Shape of road helped water to drain off and away

Nucleus (fine concrete of gravel and lime)

Stone at edge of road provides support

Subsoil

Cross-section of a Roman road

ROMAN ROADS

The ancient Romans were the first great road-building civilization. About 50,000 miles (80,000 km) of paved roads spanned the Roman Empire. These roads let armies march across the empire at up to 20 miles (30 km) a day. The best Roman roads were made of layers of stone and gravel topped with flat slabs. Remains of Roman roads, such as the Appian Way in Italy and the Fosse Way in England, can still be seen today.

CITY STREETS

Roads in early settlements often had soft ground. The wheels of wagons and carts would cut into it, forming deep ruts. This created a need for streets with harder surfaces. The oldest paved streets date from around 4000 BCE, and have been found in the Sumerian city of Ur (in present-day Iraq). By 2600 BCE, people were building paved streets in the cities of Harappa and Mohenjo-daro in the Indus Valley. Within a thousand years, paved roads became common in the Middle East and Greece. Some of these ancient streets survive to the present day.

ROYAL ROAD

In the 5th century BCE, King Darius I of Persia (present-day Iran) completed an ancient highway called the Royal Road. It linked major cities of the vast Persian Empire. The road connected the Persian capital city of Susa with the city of Sardis—a distance of 1,500 miles (2,500 km). The road was of vital importance to the Persian Empire, allowing armies of soldiers on foot—wielding spears, swords, and bows and arrows—to be deployed across the empire. Sending messages also became easier—a royal messenger on horseback could travel the length of the road in seven days. The same journey on foot took three months. Outposts, or inns, called *caravanserai*, were built along the route so that travelers could change horses or rest when needed.

Soldier in Persian army, from a frieze in Darius' royal palace in Susa, Iran

FROM ASIA TO EUROPE

The Silk Road was a network of trade routes that extended for 4,000 miles (6,400 km) from Southeast Asia to Europe. It passed through China, India, Persia, and the Middle East. The route was named after silk, which was the main item to be traded along it. Other goods included tea, ivory, spices, textiles, gold, silver, and precious stones. This map shows the route taken on the Silk Road by Marco Polo, a 13th-century European explorer.

TRAVELING ON A PRAYER

In Europe from the 4th century CE, many long-distance roads were established by pilgrims—people on a religious mission to visit a far-away shrine or holy place. Pilgrims walked for weeks or months to reach a shrine and often wore souvenir badges, such as this scallop shell. In some places, noblemen maintained the roads the pilgrims used. The rulers of Lombardy in Italy paid for the upkeep of part of a pilgrim route called the Via Francigena that extended from Rome to Canterbury in England.

The age of sail

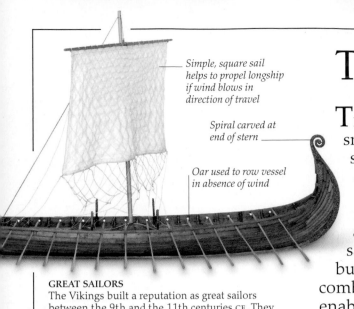

Simple, square sail helps to propel longship if wind blows in direction of travel

Spiral carved at end of stern

Oar used to row vessel in absence of wind

THE ANCIENT EGYPTIANS were navigating the Nile River in small sailing ships as early as 3500 BCE. These vessels used square sails, as did the trading ships of the ancient Greeks and Romans. Over time, sailors built bigger ships to sail over greater distances. A new kind of sail called the lateen sail was developed in the Mediterranean and the Far East around the 2nd century CE, heralding the golden age of sailing ships. From the 1100s, European ship builders began to construct vessels with a combination of square and lateen sails, enabling the vessels to make better use of the wind. These great sailing ships were the caravels and carracks, which allowed European sailors to set out on voyages of discovery—mapping oceans, opening trade routes, and discovering new lands.

GREAT SAILORS

The Vikings built a reputation as great sailors between the 9th and the 11th centuries CE. They sailed on the seas in wooden longships with square sails, navigating in open water using the position of the Sun and stars. The Vikings lived in Scandinavia, but they established settlements in nearby Britain, France, and Germany. They also made long transatlantic voyages to Greenland and North America in wooden cargo ships called *knarrs*.

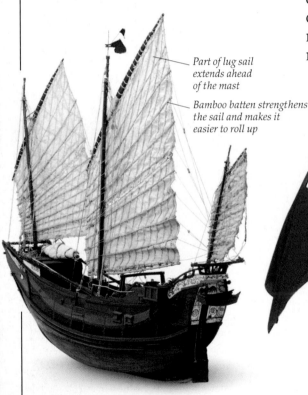

Part of lug sail extends ahead of the mast

Bamboo batten strengthens the sail and makes it easier to roll up

Red ensign, or flag, of the British Royal Navy

Mizzen mast located behind main mast

Captain's cabin

Rudder used for steering ship

Replica of HMB *Endeavour*, a barque from 1768

INTO THE WIND

The Chinese were sailing in the open seas as early as the 2nd century CE in vessels called junks. These junks dominated the waters of the Far East for nearly 2,000 years and are still popular today. While large war junks patrolled the rivers and coastlines of China, protecting the land from pirates and invaders, tradesmen transported their goods between trading posts in merchant junks, like the one above. Junks had large, fan-shaped sails called lug sails mounted on three or more masts. Unlike square sails, which worked only if the wind was behind the ship, lug sails could be pointed inward, along the length of the vessel, and at a slight angle to the wind. This allowed the ships to sail into the wind.

MANY SAILS

Throughout history, different types of sail have propelled ships, but the basic science behind sailing has remained the same. As the sail fills with air, pressure builds up behind it. The difference between the air pressure in front of the sail and behind it sucks it forward, moving the ship through the water. The pressure of the keel against the water prevents the ship from tipping over or capsizing.

SQUARE SAIL
Egyptian sailors probably invented the simple, square sail as early as 3500 BCE to propel small vessels along the Nile River.

Main mast

SPRIT SAIL
By the 2nd century BCE, Greek vessels patrolled the Aegean Sea using four-sided sprit sails. The sprit extends from the main mast.

Sprit supports face of sail
Triangular shape of sail

LATEEN SAIL
The lateen sail dates to the 2nd century CE, when Roman sailors navigated the waters of the Mediterranean Sea. Lateen means Latin.

Yard mounted at an angle along mast
Boom supports sail

BERMUDA SAIL
Invented in Bermuda in the 17th century CE, the Bermuda sail is a tall, triangular sail. It is a typical part of most modern sailing ships.

Main mast, tallest on ship

Foremast

Ring used to hold astrolabe
Outer brass ring marked in degrees to read angle of the Sun or star above horizon
Rotating alidade points to the angle of the Sun or star

WHERE ARE WE?
With no landmarks to guide them, the first sailors relied on the position of the Sun and stars to navigate the open ocean. They used an instrument called a mariner's astrolabe to determine the ship's latitude—its distance north or south of the equator. The navigator held the astrolabe by the ring at the top and aligned it to the direction of the Sun or a star, viewing the object through a rotating pointer called an alidade. The altitude of the Sun or star was then read off the brass rim. With star charts and tables, the navigator would then calculate the ship's latitude.

Mariner's astrolabe

Henry the Navigator
Vasco da Gama
Ferdinand Magellan

Statues of many famous explorers are seen in the *Padrão dos Descobrimentos*, a monument in Lisbon, Portugal

DISCOVERING NEW WORLDS
In the 15th and 16th centuries, European monarchs tasked sailors such as Christopher Columbus and Vasco da Gama to build sailing ships and explore the world. The caravels they built were large enough to sail the seas, but small enough to navigate close inshore. Carracks were larger, ocean-going vessels. Both kinds of ship had three masts, although early caravels had two masts, and later carracks had four masts. The vessels made many long voyages in the open oceans—these took Columbus to America and Vasco da Gama to India, helping them establish new trade routes and spread European culture.

FULL SAIL AHEAD
On August 28, 1768, Captain James Cook and his crew set sail from England to the uncharted southern oceans aboard a Royal Navy research vessel called HM Bark *Endeavour*. The *Endeavour* belonged to a class of ship known as a barque, or bark. This had three or more masts and a combination of different sails. Cook and his crew spent two years at sea, charting the waters around Tahiti, Australia, and New Zealand.

Running on steam

Beam rocks up and down

Crankshaft uses rocking motion of beam to move flywheel

Sealed cylinder contains piston that moves up and down

Rotating flywheel produced power that operated the water pumps

MOVING WITH STEAM
Engineers Thomas Newcomen and James Watt built the first engines to harness the power of steam. These were not invented to pull trains, but to power industrial machinery, particularly to pump water out of mines in Europe. This is a replica of the steam engine built by James Watt in 1769. The engine worked by using the pressure of steam to force a large piston up and down inside a sealed cylinder. The moving piston was connected to a beam that moved a crankshaft, which, in turn, drove a flywheel. Watt's engine would have been too heavy and inefficient to power a locomotive.

THE ADVENT OF THE STEAM ENGINE in the 18th century revolutionized transportation more than any other invention since the wheel. Before steam engines, all transportation was powered by human and animal muscles, or by using sails to catch the wind. Steam-powered passenger locomotives become a reality in 1829 with the *Rocket*, built by George and Robert Stephenson. Their breakthrough marked the beginning of the railroads as a form of public transportation. The success of the *Rocket* built on the pioneering work of engineers such as Nicolas-Joseph Cugnot and his steam tractor—the first vehicle to be run by steam—and Richard Trevithick and his *Catch-Me-Who-Can*, an early steam-powered locomotive.

Firebox produces hot gases by burning coal, and gases rise into inner boiler tubes

Inner boiler tube runs through boiler, and is surrounded by water that when heated changes into steam

Regulator valve controls amount of steam delivered to pistons

Area around boiler tube is filled with steam and water

Connecting rod converts to-and-fro motion of piston into turning motion of wheels

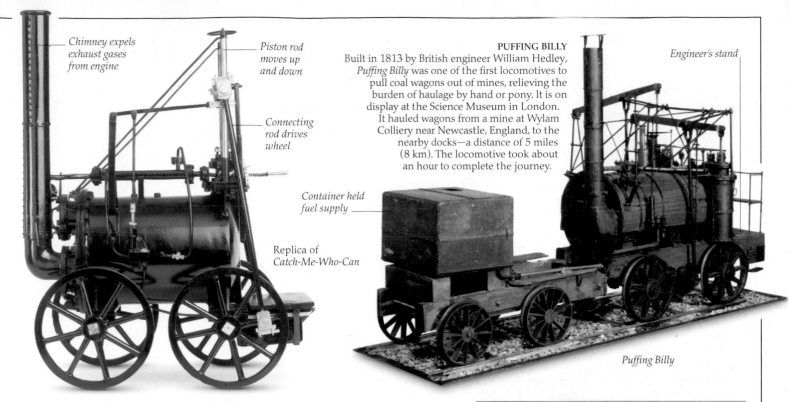

Chimney expels exhaust gases from engine

Piston rod moves up and down

Connecting rod drives wheel

Replica of Catch-Me-Who-Can

PUFFING BILLY
Built in 1813 by British engineer William Hedley, *Puffing Billy* was one of the first locomotives to pull coal wagons out of mines, relieving the burden of haulage by hand or pony. It is on display at the Science Museum in London. It hauled wagons from a mine at Wylam Colliery near Newcastle, England, to the nearby docks—a distance of 5 miles (8 km). The locomotive took about an hour to complete the journey.

Engineer's stand

Container held fuel supply

Puffing Billy

THE FIRST LOCOMOTIVES
Before steam power, miners used ponies to haul coal wagons out of mines, sometimes along rail tracks. British engineer Richard Trevithick realized that a steam-powered vehicle would make the job much easier. He built the first steam locomotive in 1804. Four years later, he built his most famous locomotive—named *Catch-Me-Who-Can* because it appeared to chase itself around its circular track. Trevithick's inventions were vital in the early development of powered railroads, which took place in Britain—the country where the Industrial Revolution was most advanced.

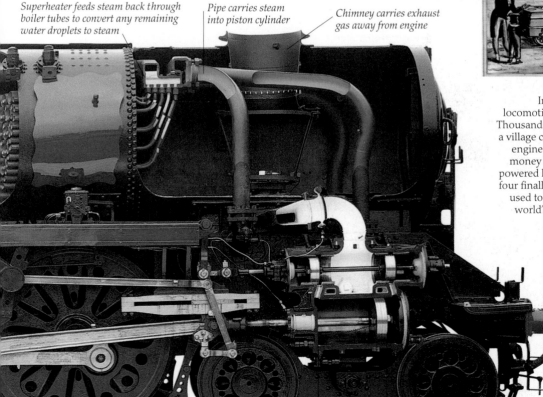

Superheater feeds steam back through boiler tubes to convert any remaining water droplets to steam

Pipe carries steam into piston cylinder

Chimney carries exhaust gas away from engine

Cutout view of a steam locomotive

Piston cylinder

Piston moves to and fro

RAINHILL TRIALS
In 1829, the Rainhill Trials were held to select a locomotive for the new Liverpool-Manchester Railway. Thousands of people from across England descended on a village called Rainhill to see the best designs of British engineers compete in the contest and claim the prize money of £500. A total of 10 horse-drawn and steam-powered locomotives entered the competition, but only four finally competed. The winner was the *Rocket*. It was used to open the Liverpool-Manchester Railway—the world's first intercity passenger railroad—a year later.

HOW DOES IT WORK?
A steam engine converts the heat energy released from burning coal into kinetic (movement) energy of the moving locomotive. Burning coal in the firebox produces hot gases that pass through tubes running in a water-filled boiler. The hot gases heat the water into steam, before escaping through the chimney. The steam passes into the piston cylinder via a regulator valve that controls the amount of steam delivered to the pistons. The force of the steam moves the pistons to and fro, turning the wheels through a connecting rod. Spent steam leaves the engine through the chimney.

Steaming ahead

THE INVENTION OF THE STEAM ENGINE revolutionized transportation on land and water. By the early 1800s, engineers were building boats with steam-powered paddle wheels to ferry passengers up and down the rivers of France, Britain, and the US. Within a few decades, powerful engines were helping huge iron steamships—such as the *Great Western*—cross the oceans, transporting people and cargo between continents. Around the same time, the success of the British steam railroads served as the model for rail travel around the world, from America to Australia.

Exhaust steam passes out of funnel

Model of SS Sirius

Paddle wheel moves ship forward

CROSSING THE ATLANTIC
The *SS Sirius* was the first ship to cross the Atlantic Ocean under continuous steam power. The 700-ton (639-metric-ton) steamer bound for New York left the Irish port of Cork on April 4, 1838, and took 19 days to complete the journey. By 1840, British steamships were regularly crossing the Atlantic Ocean, carrying thousands of people bound for the US in search of a better life.

Engineer's cab on top of the engine provides a clear view of track

AMERICAN RAILROADS
In the early days of American rail travel, the different parts for locomotives, train cars, and tracks were built in Britain and shipped to the US. By the mid-1830s, American engineers began to build their own locomotives by customizing British designs. One modification was the distinctive V-shaped cowcatcher at the front of the locomotives, seen on this *Jupiter* replica. Since the American railroad crossed open plains, cows and buffalo could easily wander on to the tracks. The cowcatcher swept the animals aside and stopped them from derailing the train.

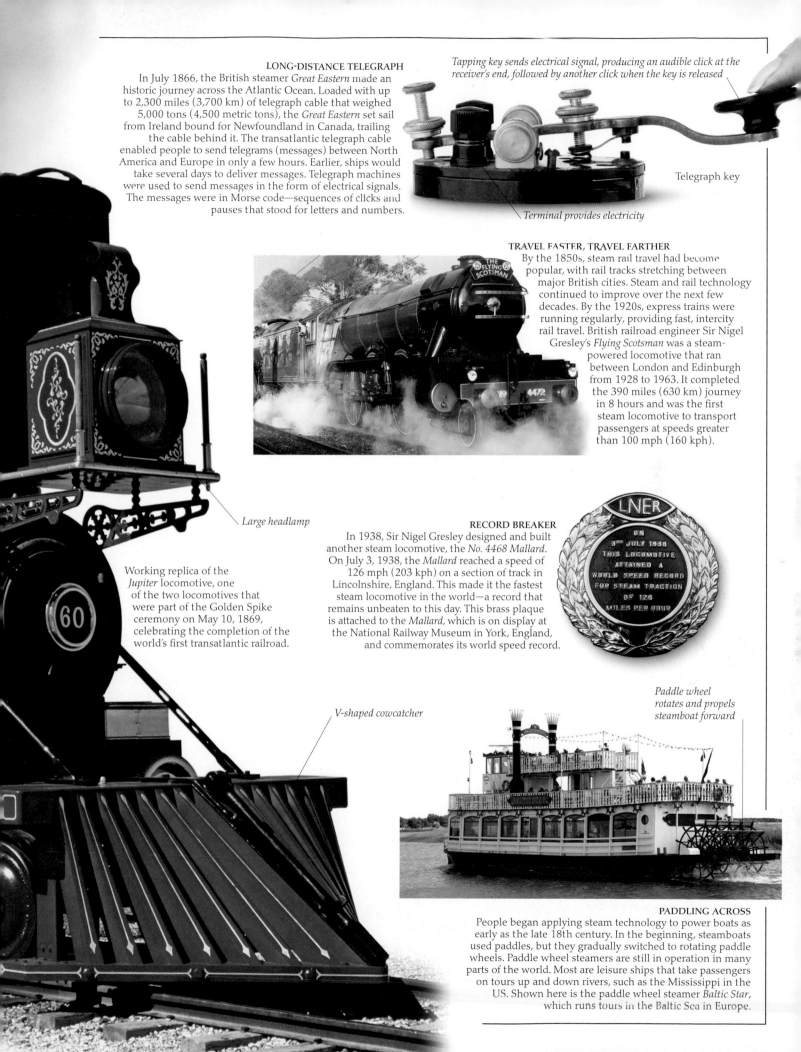

LONG-DISTANCE TELEGRAPH

In July 1866, the British steamer *Great Eastern* made an historic journey across the Atlantic Ocean. Loaded with up to 2,300 miles (3,700 km) of telegraph cable that weighed 5,000 tons (4,500 metric tons), the *Great Eastern* set sail from Ireland bound for Newfoundland in Canada, trailing the cable behind it. The transatlantic telegraph cable enabled people to send telegrams (messages) between North America and Europe in only a few hours. Earlier, ships would take several days to deliver messages. Telegraph machines were used to send messages in the form of electrical signals. The messages were in Morse code—sequences of clicks and pauses that stood for letters and numbers.

Tapping key sends electrical signal, producing an audible click at the receiver's end, followed by another click when the key is released

Telegraph key

Terminal provides electricity

TRAVEL FASTER, TRAVEL FARTHER

By the 1850s, steam rail travel had become popular, with rail tracks stretching between major British cities. Steam and rail technology continued to improve over the next few decades. By the 1920s, express trains were running regularly, providing fast, intercity rail travel. British railroad engineer Sir Nigel Gresley's *Flying Scotsman* was a steam-powered locomotive that ran between London and Edinburgh from 1928 to 1963. It completed the 390 miles (630 km) journey in 8 hours and was the first steam locomotive to transport passengers at speeds greater than 100 mph (160 kph).

Large headlamp

Working replica of the *Jupiter* locomotive, one of the two locomotives that were part of the Golden Spike ceremony on May 10, 1869, celebrating the completion of the world's first transatlantic railroad.

RECORD BREAKER

In 1938, Sir Nigel Gresley designed and built another steam locomotive, the *No. 4468 Mallard*. On July 3, 1938, the *Mallard* reached a speed of 126 mph (203 kph) on a section of track in Lincolnshire, England. This made it the fastest steam locomotive in the world—a record that remains unbeaten to this day. This brass plaque is attached to the *Mallard*, which is on display at the National Railway Museum in York, England, and commemorates its world speed record.

LNER

ON 3RD JULY 1938 THIS LOCOMOTIVE ATTAINED A WORLD SPEED RECORD FOR STEAM TRACTION OF 126 MILES PER HOUR

Paddle wheel rotates and propels steamboat forward

V-shaped cowcatcher

PADDLING ACROSS

People began applying steam technology to power boats as early as the late 18th century. In the beginning, steamboats used paddles, but they gradually switched to rotating paddle wheels. Paddle wheel steamers are still in operation in many parts of the world. Most are leisure ships that take passengers on tours up and down rivers, such as the Mississippi in the US. Shown here is the paddle wheel steamer *Baltic Star*, which runs tours in the Baltic Sea in Europe.

Opening up the land

BEFORE THE COMING OF RAILROADS, horses and boats were the main means of long-distance transportation. Horse-drawn stagecoaches were slow compared with steam trains. Journeys that took all day by stagecoach took just a few hours by train. Rail travel was also cheap because many people could be transported at one time on a train. During the 19th century, railroad networks opened around the world. In Europe, railroads connected existing cities, while in North America, railroads stimulated the growth of new settlements. In 1840, there were only 40 miles (65 km) of railroad in the US. Twenty years later, the number had grown to 29,000 miles (46,500 km). Railroads opened up the entire continent, joining the East and West coasts by 1869. The technology behind railroads continued to evolve—iron rails gave way to those made of steel, and engineering marvels, such as bridges and tunnels, became commonplace.

Replica stagecoach

STAGECOACH TRAVEL
Before rail travel became popular, people traveled in horse-drawn vehicles, from simple wooden carts to more comfortable carriages. In the 16th century, four-wheeled stagecoaches with cushions and polished wood made traveling across Europe more agreeable. Wealthy people owned personal vehicles, but others used coach-for-rent services—the historical equivalent of modern taxis. Public stagecoaches, meanwhile, were like today's long-distance buses, traveling along fixed routes and making scheduled stops called stages.

Barges on China's Grand Canal

ON THE CANALS
China's Grand Canal is the longest canal in the world, with a total length of 1,103 miles (1,776 km). The oldest parts of the canal date back to the 5th century BCE. Before railroads, canals were the most important transportation routes in China. Transporting cargo and people on these waterways was faster than by land because road systems were poorly developed.

THE AMERICAN RAILROADS

Between 1863 and 1869, gangs of laborers built the world's first transcontinental railroad, linking the East and West coasts of the US. The gangs moved from one place to the next as they completed sections of track, tunnels, and bridges, living in temporary camps or renting rooms in nearby towns. They were responsible for the rapid expansion of railroads in the US, which created new settlements in the natural wilderness of the Great Plains. Many cities west of the Mississippi River, such as Dallas and Kansas City, came about as a result of the railroad expansion.

First-class railroad ticket, 1923

TICKET TO RIDE

From the early 1830s, railroad operators started to offer day trips, such as outings to the beach and the countryside. For the first time, ordinary people began traveling on pleasure trips and vacations. Wealthier passengers traveled in first-class compartments, which had padded seats, extra legroom, and private toilets. Second-class passengers sometimes sat in open wagons with less comfort and space, while the packed third-class cars were standing-room only.

Irish laborers working on a track, April 1869

MARVELS OF ENGINEERING

Building tunnels and bridges was a feat that required a great deal of engineering skill. Bridges and tunnels took railroad lines over rivers and ravines and through mountains. Workers moved millions of tons of rock and soil by hand, using nothing but picks, shovels, and wheelbarrows. Engineers made their name designing bridges and tunnels for railroads. Alexander Acatos, for instance, designed the bridge seen above—the Landwasser Viaduct, a 213-ft- (65-m-) high bridge in the Swiss Alps.

THE ORIENT EXPRESS

The *Orient Express* was one of the most famous luxury train services. It opened in 1883, connecting Paris, France, with Constantinople (Istanbul), Turkey, and continued to run until 2009. The *Orient Express* offered the same services as a top-class hotel. Passengers could enjoy five-star cuisine in the magnificent dining cars and then relax in comfortable sleeping cars designed by George Pullman—the pioneer of luxury train travel.

Above and below

CITIES GREW RAPIDLY in the 19th century. People flocked from the countryside and businesses multiplied—as did traffic on the roads. Congestion in the streets became a major urban problem. Engineers attempted to solve this by building railroad lines in underground tunnels for a new system of public transportation. The first underground railroad opened in London in 1863, and by 1880, it was carrying 40 million passengers a year. Steam-driven engines were used initially, but these eventually gave way to electric locomotives. The success of London's underground electric railroad spurred the development of similar systems in cities such as Paris and Budapest. Electric power was also used beyond the railroads—electrically powered vehicles on the roads helped public transportation become popular in the early 20th century in many parts of the world, such as the US.

Spring-loaded frame called a pantograph receives current from overhead wires

Model of an electric locomotive

ELECTRIC POWER
The invention of the electric motor solved the problem of smoke-filled tunnels in subways. From 1890 onward, steam-driven locomotives were gradually replaced by ones powered by electric motors. In the underground tunnels, electric current for the motors was supplied through an extra rail. Above ground, too, steam trains began to be replaced by electric trains in the early 1900s. Electric trains that ran above ground could receive the current either from a rail or from wires hanging above the track.

STEAMY SUBWAYS
The first tunnels for London's underground railroad network were dug using a "cut and cover" method. First, a road was dug up. Then a tunnel was built in the trench. Finally, the tunnel was covered and the road surface was laid on top. When the subways opened, trains were hauled by steam locomotives. Smoke and steam from the locomotives spread through the tunnels. Passengers traveled in a choking, sooty fog. Despite this problem, traveling underground was far quicker and more convenient than traveling on London's congested streets.

A 19th-century illustration of a section of a subway station in London

Steam locomotive entering station

Tunnel lined with brick

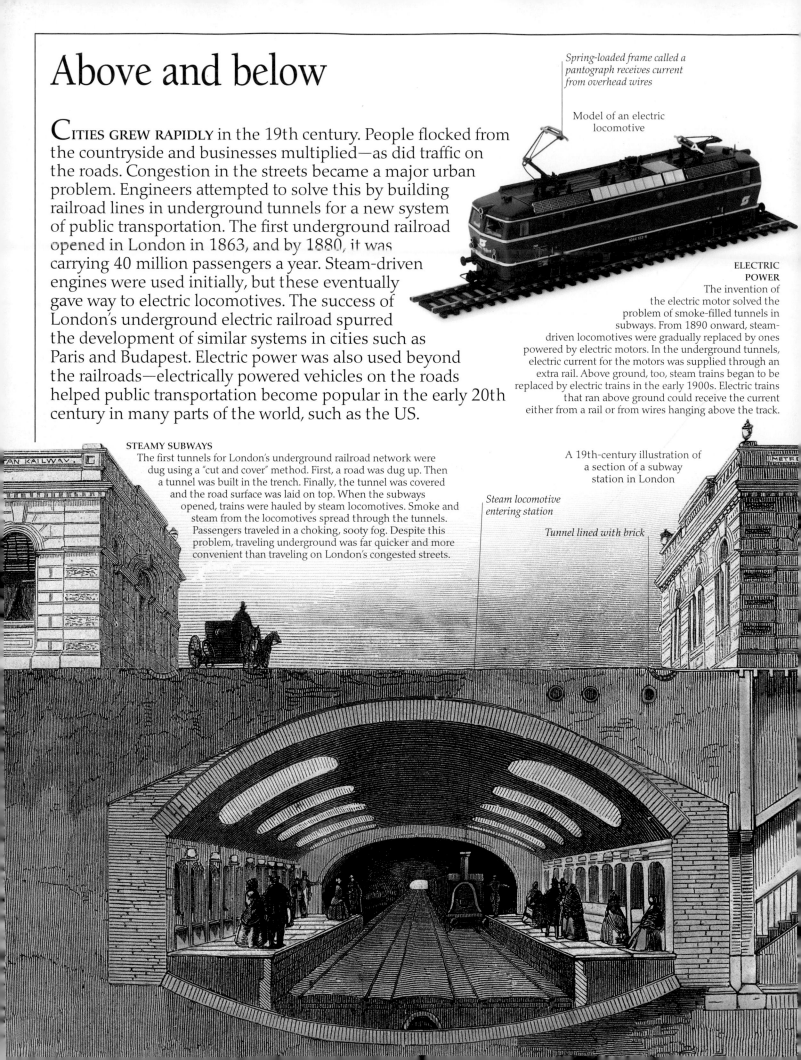

TROLLEY BUSES
In the late 1800s, several inventors built vehicles powered by electricity. One such vehicle was the trolley bus—it had spring-loaded trolley poles on top to draw current from wires suspended above the roads. The German *Electromote* was the world's first trolley bus, and it ran for the first time in 1882. This crowd has gathered to watch the last trolley bus in service in London, in 1962.

RUNNING ON CABLES
In the early 1800s, wagons in mines and quarries sometimes had to be hauled up hills too steep for locomotives to climb. The wagons were hauled by cables pulled by stationary steam engines. Tracks using cables were eventually used to pull trains and trams—these "cable cars" are now found in many parts of the world. The cable cars of San Francisco started operating in 1873 and have become a well-known feature of the city. These cable cars are pulled along by cables under the hilly streets of the city. In some cable railroads, two cars are linked together. The weight of one car going downhill balances the weight of the other going uphill. This is called a funicular railroad.

Cable car on an airline poster promoting San Francisco as a destination

IT TAKES A TOKEN
Some underground railroad systems issued tokens to pay for travel. The New York Subway is the world's fourth busiest underground railroad. It issued a series of different tokens from the 1950s to 2003. The tokens were punched or engraved with distinctive shapes and many were kept by collectors instead of being used for travel.

New York Subway tokens

FLOATING TRAM
The German city of Wuppertal chose a novel way to build a railroad. The trains, which are electrically powered, hang from a rail suspended 39 ft (12 m) above the ground. Called the Wuppertal *Schwebebahn* (floating tram), this network has been running almost continuously since 1901, when the first track opened. Now, the two-car trains carry up to 82,000 passengers a day at an average speed of 17 mph (27 kph).

ELEVATING PEOPLE
In the late 1800s, cities in the US were becoming crowded and began to spread outward and upward—the first skyscrapers were built during this period. Elevators were a crucial part of every skyscraper. Early elevators were hoisted by ropes or cables, and they were used to carry only freight, since they were considered too dangerous for people to travel in. If the rope or cable broke, the elevator car would crash to the ground. In 1852, American engineer Elisha Otis invented the safety elevator. If the cable holding it up broke, the elevator car would not fall. At the 1854 New York World's Fair, he demonstrated his machine by traveling in it while an assistant cut the cable holding it up. It did not fall because safety brakes locked the machine to the sides of the vertical shaft it was in. Otis's elevator made it possible for people to live in tall buildings—sparking the growth of the modern skyscraper.

Safety brake stops car from falling

Rope is cut by Otis's assistant

Taking to the skies

CHINESE SOLDIERS made the first manned flights around 3,000 years ago, flying on giant kites to spy on enemies. Over the millennia, people experimented with flight, strapping on wings and lunging into the air—often fatally. In the 15th century, Italian scholar Leonardo da Vinci conceived a flying machine that could mimic the flapping wings of a bird. The flapping-wing idea took a long time to die. It was still alive when the first lighter-than-air balloon took to the skies in 1783. This paved the way for pioneers, such as British engineer George Cayley, who identified the forces acting on a wing. He realized that the future of human flight lay with neither flapping wings nor balloons, but with the fixed wings of a glider.

THE PIONEERS
Joseph-Michel and Jacques-Étienne Montgolfier were the inventors of the hot-air balloon and pioneers of human flight. Their balloons were filled with air heated by burning straw kept in a pit below each balloon. They made several test flights with animals as passengers, before sending two pilots—Jean-François Pilâtre de Rozier and François Laurent d'Arlandes—into the skies above Paris on November 21, 1783.

Stamp depicting Montgolfier brothers

BALLOON SCIENCE
This hot-air balloon is able to fly because warm air rises in cold air. Smoke rises above a fire for the same reason. The air inside the balloon expands when it is heated by the burner. As the air expands, it becomes less dense—and therefore lighter—than the colder air outside the balloon. If the air in the balloon becomes hot enough and light enough, the balloon rises. Some balloons are filled with lighter-than-air gases, such as helium, instead of hot air.

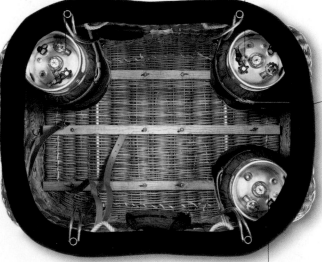

Tap for drawing liquid propane for blast-flame burner

Tap for drawing propane gas for pilot-light burner

Wooden struts reinforce floor

Burner frame

Heating coils

Wicker basket

Propane canister

Blast-flame burner sends a blast of heated air into the balloon

Propane burner

Wicker basket is light, but strong enough to absorb shock of landing

Pilot-light burner

Set of burners

Thin pipe supplies propane gas to pilot-light burner

Thick pipe supplies liquid propane to blast-flame burner

BALLOON TECHNOLOGY
Modern hot-air balloons use burners fueled by propane. Canisters of propane are carried in a wicker basket and are connected to the burners by pipes. The pilot-light burner works constantly to keep a series of coils heated. Liquid propane flows through the heated coils and vaporizes into propane gas. The gas rushes out and is ignited when the blast-flame burner is turned on. This blows hot air into the narrow end of the balloon, making the balloon rise.

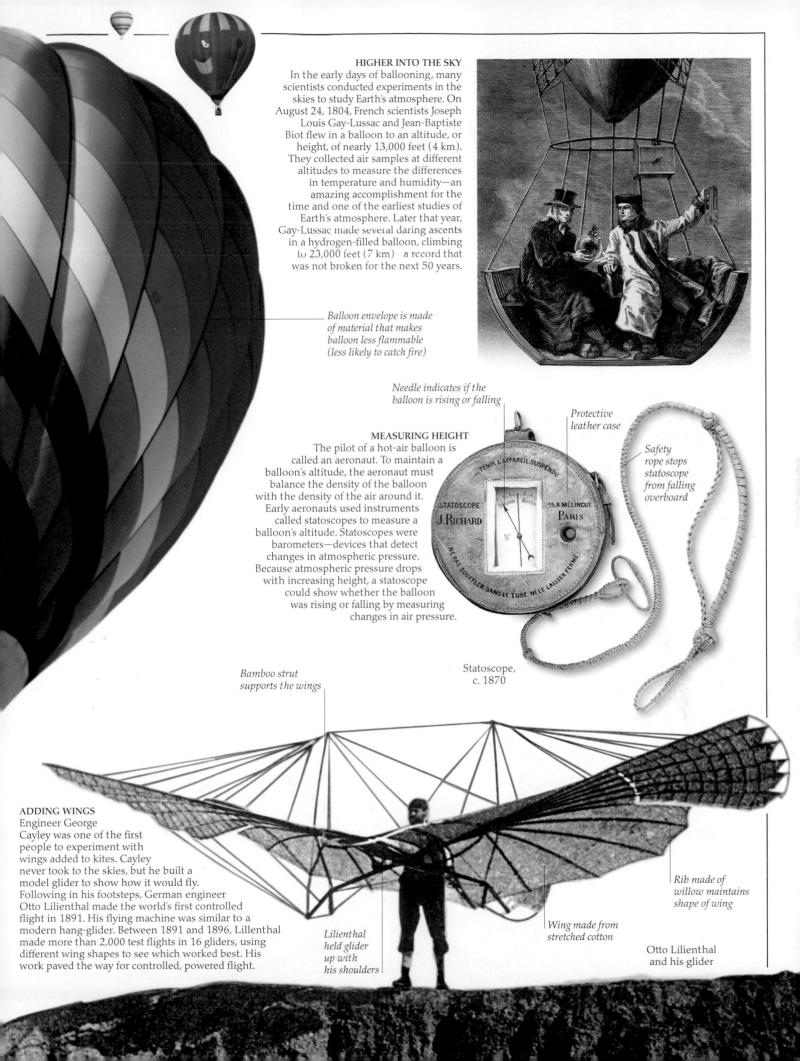

HIGHER INTO THE SKY

In the early days of ballooning, many scientists conducted experiments in the skies to study Earth's atmosphere. On August 24, 1804, French scientists Joseph Louis Gay-Lussac and Jean-Baptiste Biot flew in a balloon to an altitude, or height, of nearly 13,000 feet (4 km). They collected air samples at different altitudes to measure the differences in temperature and humidity—an amazing accomplishment for the time and one of the earliest studies of Earth's atmosphere. Later that year, Gay-Lussac made several daring ascents in a hydrogen-filled balloon, climbing to 23,000 feet (7 km)—a record that was not broken for the next 50 years.

Balloon envelope is made of material that makes balloon less flammable (less likely to catch fire)

Needle indicates if the balloon is rising or falling

Protective leather case

Safety rope stops statoscope from falling overboard

MEASURING HEIGHT

The pilot of a hot-air balloon is called an aeronaut. To maintain a balloon's altitude, the aeronaut must balance the density of the balloon with the density of the air around it. Early aeronauts used instruments called statoscopes to measure a balloon's altitude. Statoscopes were barometers—devices that detect changes in atmospheric pressure. Because atmospheric pressure drops with increasing height, a statoscope could show whether the balloon was rising or falling by measuring changes in air pressure.

Statoscope, c. 1870

Bamboo strut supports the wings

ADDING WINGS

Engineer George Cayley was one of the first people to experiment with wings added to kites. Cayley never took to the skies, but he built a model glider to show how it would fly. Following in his footsteps, German engineer Otto Lilienthal made the world's first controlled flight in 1891. His flying machine was similar to a modern hang-glider. Between 1891 and 1896, Lilienthal made more than 2,000 test flights in 16 gliders, using different wing shapes to see which worked best. His work paved the way for controlled, powered flight.

Rib made of willow maintains shape of wing

Wing made from stretched cotton

Lilienthal held glider up with his shoulders

Otto Lilienthal and his glider

Internal combustion engine

B<small>Y THE MID-19TH CENTURY</small>, vehicles driven by steam engines had been on the roads for almost 100 years. These carriages remained rare and unpopular, however, because their engines were bulky and inefficient, and they belched out thick, black smoke. In 1860, Belgian engineer Étienne Lenoir built a new type of engine that burned coal gas as fuel, and was small but powerful enough to drive a wooden cart. It was the world's first internal combustion engine—so called because it combusted, or burned, fuel inside cylinders. The internal combustion engine paved the way for the invention of a range of vehicles such as automobiles, trucks, motorcycles, powerboats, and airplanes.

NIKOLAUS OTTO

Nikolaus Otto improved the design of Lenoir's engine, and in 1876, he built an engine that worked on a four-stroke cycle (see p. 29). This made Otto's engine far more efficient than Lenoir's creation, which used three strokes. With the help of fellow German engineer Gottlieb Daimler, Otto later adapted his engine to burn gasoline instead of coal gas. His invention eventually became the basis of all modern internal combustion engines.

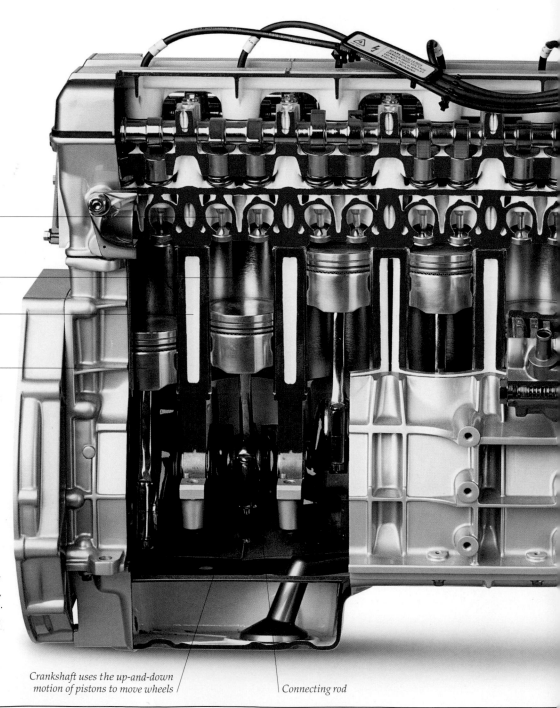

Intake, or inlet, valve opens to let fuel–air mixture into cylinder

Combustion chamber houses the fuel–air mixture

Water jacket surrounds combustion chamber, keeping it cool

Piston uses energy produced by combustion of fuel to turn crankshaft

Crankshaft uses the up-and-down motion of pistons to move wheels

Connecting rod

ENGINE ANATOMY

The internal combustion engine burns fuel—such as gasoline—inside chambers called cylinders. The cylinders are tubes cut through a solid chunk of metal called the cylinder block. Modern gas-based engines have anywhere between one and 12 cylinders. In most engines, the cylinders are set in a straight line, such as in this "Straight-6" engine from a Jaguar car. While the engine is running, the fuel is mixed with air and an electric spark ignites it, causing it to explode and expand rapidly. This forces the pistons to move up and down inside the series of cylinders, resulting in the rotation of a metal rod called the crankshaft. This, in turn, moves the wheels of the vehicle.

FOUR STROKES

Nikolaus Otto's engine was a four-stroke engine, the same kind used by nearly all modern cars. Every piston completes four steps in a cycle—these are the four strokes that power the engine. A piston moves up and down twice in every cycle, turning the crankshaft each time.

Fuel–air mixture injected into cylinder

Piston rises and compresses fuel–air mixture

Spark plug

Inlet valve open

Piston moves down, pulling fuel–air mixture into cylinder

In the intake stroke, a mixture of fuel and air is sucked into the cylinder through the inlet valve

Inlet valve closed

In the compression stroke, the fuel–air mixture is compressed to a high pressure

Spark plug ignites fuel

Explosive expansion of burning fuel forces piston downwards

Crankshaft turns due to movement of piston

In the power stroke, an electrical spark ignites the fuel and the resulting explosion drives the piston downwards

Waste gases pushed out

Outlet valve open

Piston rises again

In the exhaust stroke, the rising piston expels waste gases through the exhaust valve

RUNNING ON DIESEL

In 1892, German engineer Rudolf Diesel invented a new type of engine that ran on a cheap, low-grade fuel, now called diesel in his honor. Diesel engines compress only air during the compression stroke. Fuel is added later. Such engines do not have a spark plug—the hot, compressed air ignites the fuel. Diesel engines are more efficient and produce more power than gasoline engines, so they are used to power mainly heavy vehicles such as trucks and buses. But they are expensive to manufacture and maintain.

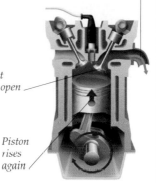

Early diesel-powered truck made by Edwin Foden, Sons & Co., a British company

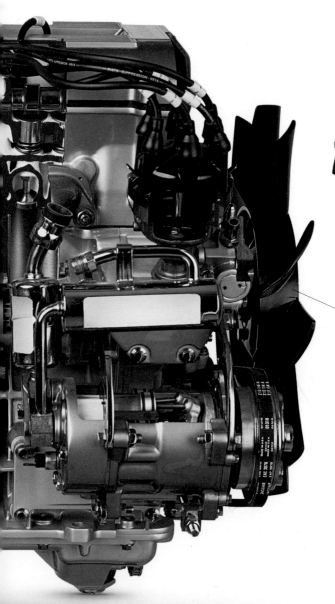

Fan keeps the engine cool by moving air through the radiator, which forms part of the engine's cooling system

Crankshaft at center is connected to airplane body and is stationary

Connecting rod joins piston inside cylinder to crankshaft

Inlet pipe channels fuel–air mixture into cylinder

Valve lets fuel in and waste gases out

Rotary engine built by the Seguin brothers

Crankcase moves around crankshaft

PISTONS ALL AROUND

The internal combustion engine was the missing link in the quest for powered flight. Steam engines were too heavy and inefficient for flying machines, but a compact, powerful internal combustion engine was ideal. Orville and Wilbur Wright built the first gas-powered flying machine in the early years of the 20th century, just a few decades after the invention of the internal combustion engine. In 1909, the Seguin brothers of France improved their design and built a rotary engine. This engine had pistons arranged around a central crankshaft, and the entire cylinder block rotated around it. The engine turned the propeller of an airplane at high speeds.

On two wheels

ON YOUR BIKE

Developed in 1870 by British inventor James Starley, the *Penny Farthing* was the first two-wheeled vehicle to be called a bicycle. Since it did not have a chain to transfer the pedal movement to the wheel, the pedals were fixed and moved the wheel directly. So to cycle fast, the wheel had to be enormous. The large wheel also helped the bicycle roll more easily over rough roads.

Penny Farthing

Rubber tire

Pushing the pedal turned the wheel

BICYCLE DESIGN CAN BE TRACED back to 1817, when German inventor Baron Karl von Drais built a two-wheeled vehicle called the *Draisienne*, which a rider could push along the ground with his or her feet. By the 1880s, bicycle manufacturers were building pedal-powered machines with pneumatic, or air-filled, tires, making cycling more efficient and comfortable. Bicycles evolved a step further in the late 1800s with the invention of the gasoline engine. In fact, the earliest gas-powered vehicles were essentially motorized bicycles, or "motorcycles."

THE COMING OF MOTORCYCLES

Bicycle manufacturers throughout Europe and the United States were quick to realize the significance of gas power and adapted their designs to include an engine. As gasoline engines became more powerful in the 20th century, the motorcycle industry spread around the world. Some companies, such as Harley-Davidson, have been building motorcycles since 1905. Today, the market is dominated by Japanese companies, such as Honda, Kawasaki, and Suzuki.

The *Petroleum Reitwagen* was the world's first gas-powered motorcycle. German engineers Gottlieb Daimler and Wilhelm Maybach built the *Reitwagen* in 1885. It had a top speed of 7 mph (11 kph).

Royal Enfield motorcycle, 1914

A company called Royal Enfield dominated the British motorcycle industry from the early 1900s, supplying military motorcycles during World Wars I and II. Royal Enfield continues to build motorcycles from its headquarters in India, making it the world's oldest motorcycle manufacturer.

Maurice Garin seen on the cover of French magazine *Le Petit Journal*, winning the 1901 Paris–Brest bicycle race

Padded seat provides comfort during long rides

CYCLING TO VICTORY

Bicycle racing became popular in the late 1800s. The first documented bicycle race was a ¾ mile (1.2 km) event at Parc de Saint-Cloud in Paris, France, in 1868. Eventually, cycle races were included as events in the first modern Olympic Games in Athens, Greece, in 1896. The world's most famous bicycle race is the Tour de France, which was inaugurated in 1903. This race covers nearly 2,250 miles (3,600 km) in about 20 days.

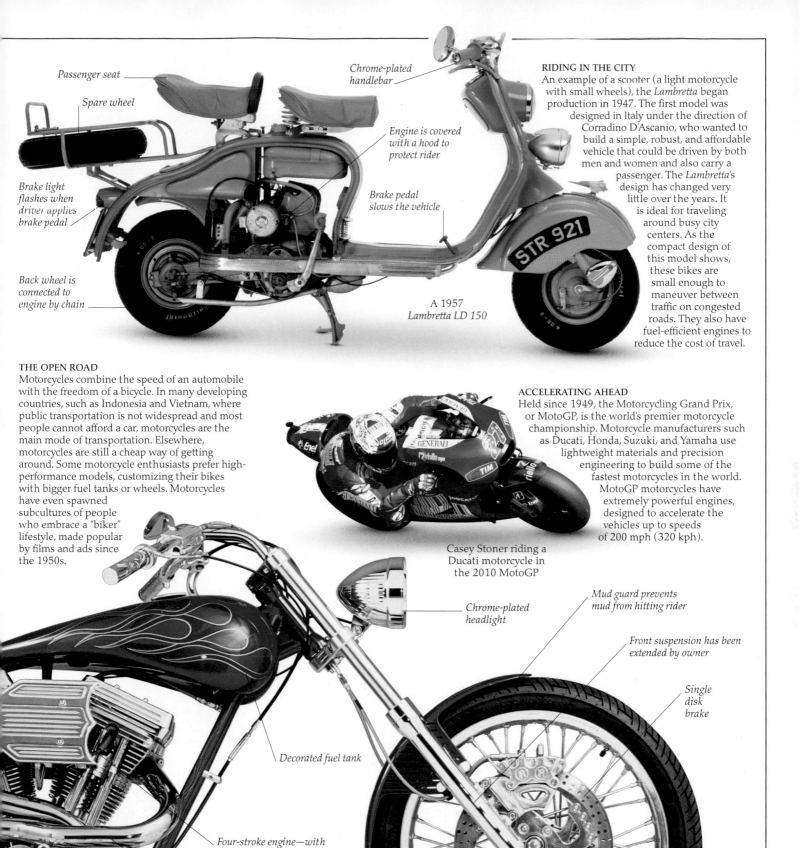

Passenger seat

Spare wheel

Chrome-plated handlebar

Brake light flashes when driver applies brake pedal

Engine is covered with a hood to protect rider

Brake pedal slows the vehicle

Back wheel is connected to engine by chain

STR 921

A 1957 *Lambretta LD 150*

RIDING IN THE CITY
An example of a scooter (a light motorcycle with small wheels), the *Lambretta* began production in 1947. The first model was designed in Italy under the direction of Corradino D'Ascanio, who wanted to build a simple, robust, and affordable vehicle that could be driven by both men and women and also carry a passenger. The *Lambretta's* design has changed very little over the years. It is ideal for traveling around busy city centers. As the compact design of this model shows, these bikes are small enough to maneuver between traffic on congested roads. They also have fuel-efficient engines to reduce the cost of travel.

THE OPEN ROAD
Motorcycles combine the speed of an automobile with the freedom of a bicycle. In many developing countries, such as Indonesia and Vietnam, where public transportation is not widespread and most people cannot afford a car, motorcycles are the main mode of transportation. Elsewhere, motorcycles are still a cheap way of getting around. Some motorcycle enthusiasts prefer high-performance models, customizing their bikes with bigger fuel tanks or wheels. Motorcycles have even spawned subcultures of people who embrace a "biker" lifestyle, made popular by films and ads since the 1950s.

ACCELERATING AHEAD
Held since 1949, the Motorcycling Grand Prix, or MotoGP, is the world's premier motorcycle championship. Motorcycle manufacturers such as Ducati, Honda, Suzuki, and Yamaha use lightweight materials and precision engineering to build some of the fastest motorcycles in the world. MotoGP motorcycles have extremely powerful engines, designed to accelerate the vehicles up to speeds of 200 mph (320 kph).

Casey Stoner riding a Ducati motorcycle in the 2010 MotoGP

Chrome-plated headlight

Mud guard prevents mud from hitting rider

Front suspension has been extended by owner

Single disk brake

Decorated fuel tank

Four-stroke engine—with two pistons arranged in a V-shape—called a V2 engine

Chrome-plated exhaust pipe

A customized 1996 Harley-Davidson *Batt Boy* motorcycle

The automobile

IN THE MID-18TH CENTURY, engineers started to apply steam power to horse carts, building the first motorized vehicles. Étienne Lenoir built the first car with an internal combustion engine in 1860 and engineers continued to improve on his design over the next few decades. In 1885, German engineer Karl Benz made a remarkable breakthrough. He built the first practical automobile—it was not just a motorized carriage, but the first vehicle designed to produce its own power. However, early automobiles were very expensive and it was the mass production technique used by American inventor Henry Ford at the beginning of the 20th century that made cars affordable for the masses.

MOTOR PIONEER
Karl Benz designed the *Benz Victoria*—the first automobile with four wheels. It was produced in 1893. Here, Karl Benz is seen riding on it with his daughter. Benz's later model, the *Velo* of 1894, could travel at speeds of up to 20 mph (30 kph). By the end of the 19th century, Benz was one of the world's leading car manufacturers, and hundreds of hand-built *Velos* were rolling out of his workshop.

Foot warmer filled with hot coals

Gloves to keep hands warm

Set of road maps in leather index case, 1920s

High seat gives driver clear view of road ahead

Steering wheel

Throttle increases car speed

Emergency foot brake

Pedal for reversing direction of movement

Leaf spring provides suspension—cushioning the car body and passengers against impacts from road

Wooden spoke similar to that used in horse carts

EARLY CARS
The earliest automobiles were unreliable machines. Drivers found it difficult to start the engine and control the vehicle on the road. In the early 1900s, French car manufacturers, such as De Dion-Bouton and Renault, began building more practical cars. Made in 1903, De Dion-Bouton's *Model Q* was a popular car with a top speed of 30 mph (50 kph). The increasing popularity of cars led to new fashions as motorists began wearing leather headgear, gloves, and driving goggles for protection when speeding down dusty roads. Horns gradually became common for safe driving.

LUXURY CARS

In 1906, British car makers Charles Rolls and Henry Royce began manufacturing the Rolls-Royce *Silver Ghost* series of cars for the luxury market. These cars had shiny aluminum bodies and smooth-running, silent engines. Luxury cars were custom-built—with sleek designs, and hand-crafted leather and velvet interiors—for the chauffeur-driven élite and wealthy hobbyists, using the best craftsmanship and materials.

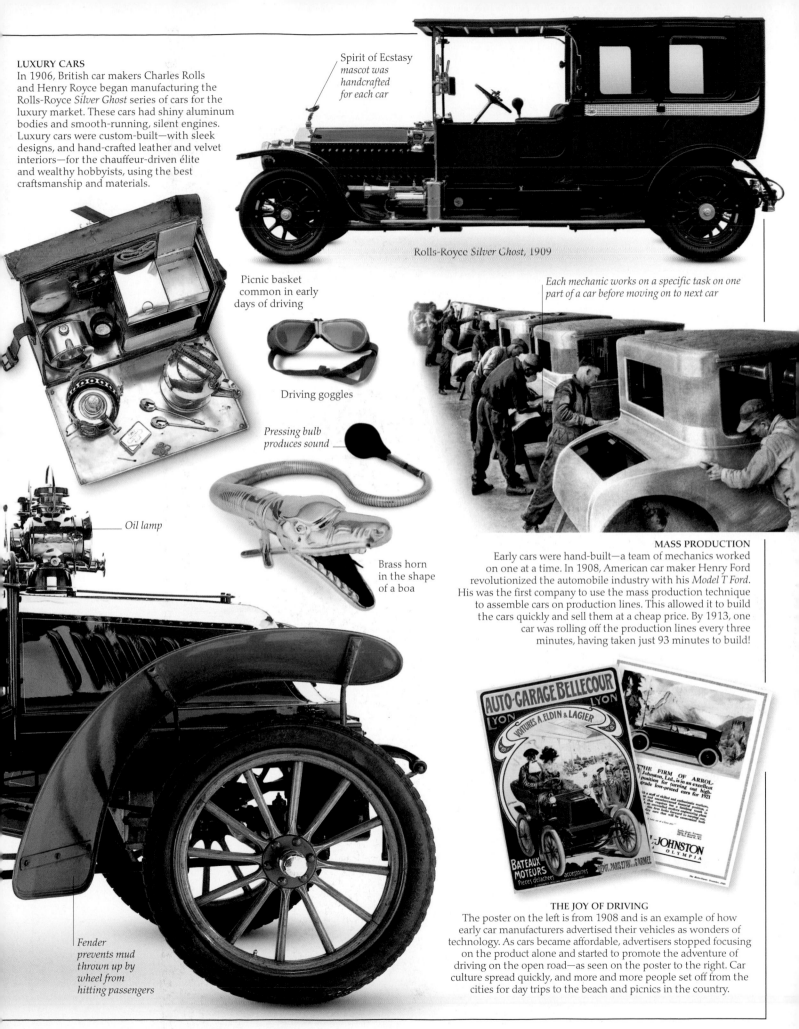

Spirit of Ecstasy mascot was handcrafted for each car

Rolls-Royce *Silver Ghost*, 1909

Picnic basket common in early days of driving

Driving goggles

Pressing bulb produces sound

Brass horn in the shape of a boa

Oil lamp

Fender prevents mud thrown up by wheel from hitting passengers

Each mechanic works on a specific task on one part of a car before moving on to next car

MASS PRODUCTION

Early cars were hand-built—a team of mechanics worked on one at a time. In 1908, American car maker Henry Ford revolutionized the automobile industry with his *Model T Ford*. His was the first company to use the mass production technique to assemble cars on production lines. This allowed it to build the cars quickly and sell them at a cheap price. By 1913, one car was rolling off the production lines every three minutes, having taken just 93 minutes to build!

THE JOY OF DRIVING

The poster on the left is from 1908 and is an example of how early car manufacturers advertised their vehicles as wonders of technology. As cars became affordable, advertisers stopped focusing on the product alone and started to promote the adventure of driving on the open road—as seen on the poster to the right. Car culture spread quickly, and more and more people set off from the cities for day trips to the beach and picnics in the country.

Powered flight

Gasoline engines for cars had revolutionized transportation on land by the early 20th century. They were also critical in the advent of powered flight. On December 17, 1903, American brothers Orville and Wilbur Wright took the first steps toward powered flight when they rose into the air in a machine called *Flyer 1*. They pulled on wires attached to the wings of the machine to twist the wings for lifting one side or the other in order to stop the plane from rolling over in the air. In doing so, they realized that their plane could make balanced turns. In the following years, engineers built larger planes with lightweight metal bodies, or fuselages, and more efficient engines to achieve greater speeds. This paved the way for breakthroughs such as the first Atlantic and Pacific crossings, and eventually, the golden age of commercial flight.

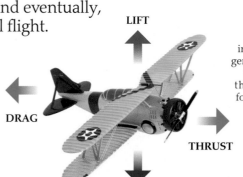

Wooden propeller

Small propeller drives pump which supplies fuel to engine

Wheel made of rubber filled with air to smooth landing

Pilot's seat made of wicker to keep plane light

FIRST FLIGHT
The Wright brothers were bicycle makers but turned their attention to flying machines in 1899. Four years later, they built *Flyer 1*. It had a wooden frame, a 12-horsepower (12-hp) engine, and wings made of wooden struts, wire, and cloth. The Wright Brothers made four flights in the plane near Kitty Hawk, North Carolina. The first flight lasted for 12 seconds, with the plane rising to just 12 ft (4 m) above the ground. Over the next five years, the Wright brothers made hundreds of test flights, developing *Flyer 1* into a more sturdy and powerful aircraft, capable of sustaining flight for longer periods.

Orville and Wilbur Wright, an artistic representation

LIFT

DRAG

THRUST

WEIGHT

THE PHYSICS OF FLIGHT
Four forces act on a plane in flight. Thrust is the force generated by the engine that pushes the plane through the air. Drag is friction—the force of air hitting the body of the aircraft that slows it down. Weight is the force of gravity pulling the aircraft down toward the ground. Lift is the force produced by air passing over the curved wings of the plane, pushing it upward.

D-1929

DOMINATING THE SKIES

Machine gun

The onset of World War I fueled the growth of the aircraft industry, as the opposing forces needed reliable aircraft that could fly into combat every day. Engineers developed more powerful engines, increasing power from 80 hp in 1914 to 400 hp by the end of the war. Early military aircraft were designed for different roles, such as bombing raids, reconnaissance, and aerial dogfights. The British *Bristol Fighter* was a multipurpose plane used for most of these roles.

Frame of plane body, or fuselage, made of lightweight spruce wood

Wire controls movement of rudder

Bristol Fighter, c. 1917

Tail rudder aligns the plane's nose

Imperial Airways poster, 1936

FLYING THE WORLD

During the 1920s and 1930s, advances in aircraft design and engine power, coupled with the development of instruments, such as altimeters and autopilots, spurred the development of the first passenger services. Imperial Airways of Britain offered flights between London's Croydon Airport and Le Bourget in Paris. In the United States, airlines such as Pan American Airways were flying passengers from coast to coast in hours rather than the days it took by train.

PIONEERING PILOTS

In the years following World War I, pioneering pilots captured the imagination of the public with epic flights around the world. In 1927, American pilot Charles Lindbergh flew solo across the Atlantic Ocean in the *Spirit of St. Louis*. Women aviators also set many records. In 1930, British pilot Amy Johnson, seen on the left, took 19.5 days to fly from England to Australia in a de Havilland *DH-60 Moth* named Jason.

FLYING BOATS

This German *Dornier Do X1A* was the largest and most powerful flying boat in the world in 1929. During the 1930s, flying boats were among the most popular types of passenger aircraft. At this time, airplanes were unreliable, their ranges were not great, and there were still not many airfields where they could land. Flying boats could take off or land anywhere on water. They could reach destinations around the world without the need for airfields. However, these aircraft were slow.

LUFT HANSA

 Hull shaped like that of boat helped aircraft to land in water

ZEPPELINS

The German Zeppelin Company was the world's leading airship, or zeppelin, manufacturer in the years following World War I. By 1920, these enormous hydrogen-filled airships were regularly carrying passengers across the Atlantic Ocean. The LZ 129 *Hindenburg*, shown here above New York City was the largest flying machine ever built, reaching 800 ft (245 m) in length—more than three times the length of a modern jumbo jet. In 1937, the *Hindenburg* burst into flames in the skies above New Jersey, marking the end of commercial airship travel.

The helicopter

THE ROTATING WINGS, OR BLADES, OF A HELICOPTER allow it to take off vertically, hover motionless in the air, and land in places where fixed-wing aircraft cannot land. The first functional helicopter was the *Focke-Wulf Fw 61*, which was built in Germany in the 1930s. It had two large rotors—one on each side. It was so stable and controllable that, in 1938, it was flown inside a covered sports stadium. A year later, Russian-born American engineer Igor Sikorsky designed the *Vought-Sikorsky VS-300*, the machine that pioneered the design now used in every helicopter—the combination of a large overhead rotor and a small tail rotor.

DA VINCI'S MACHINE
In the 1480s, Italian scientist Leonardo da Vinci designed a vertical takeoff aircraft called an aerial screw. Had it been built, it would have been 15 ft (4.5 m) across. Men standing below would have turned handles to make the whole craft rotate. Da Vinci believed that if it rotated fast enough, then it would rise into the air. He did not manage to build a working model of the screw, and scientists now believe that the craft would not have flown.

Rotor blade
of helicopter

OFF THE GROUND
French engineer Paul Cornu can be seen here in his creation—the first manned helicopter. He flew it in 1907, but only for 20 seconds, rising just 1 ft (30 cm) off the ground. Cornu's machine flew, but could not be controlled. Realizing the impracticality of his design, he abandoned it soon afterward.

Rotorcraft

Aircraft that fly by using spinning rotors are called rotorcraft. The two main types of rotorcraft are the autogyro and the helicopter.

Tail rotor stops the
aircraft from spinning
out of control

Twin-blade
main rotor

Cierva C-30
autogyro

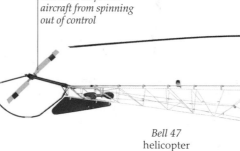

Bell 47
helicopter

AUTOGYRO
The first important breakthrough in rotorcraft came in 1923 when Spanish engineer Juan de la Cierva invented the autogyro. An autogyro uses an unpowered rotor for lift and a separate propeller for forward thrust. As the propeller moves the aircraft forward, air flows through the overhead rotor and makes it spin, creating lift for takeoff and flight.

HELICOPTER
The standard helicopter layout—with a powered main rotor on top and a small powered rotor behind the tail—was already established by 1946, when the *Bell 47* became the first helicopter to be certified for use by the general public. The pilot presses pedals to alter the thrust of the tail rotor, making the helicopter turn to the left or right.

AEROBATICS

Since helicopters can fly in any direction, they are often used to perform amazing aerial stunts. However, most helicopters cannot roll upside down or loop the loop. The *MBB Bo-105,* shown above, and *Eurocopter EC-135,* are exceptions. Unlike other helicopters in which the rotor blades are attached to the rotor by hinges, the blades of these aerobatic helicopters are fixed directly to the rotor. This makes the blades more flexible and enables these helicopters to perform rolls, loops, and other aerobatic maneuvers, just like fixed-wing aircraft.

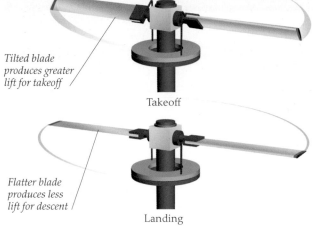

Tilted blade produces greater lift for takeoff

Takeoff

Flatter blade produces less lift for descent

Landing

FLYING UP AND DOWN

To take off, a helicopter pilot increases the engine power to bring the main rotor up to full speed. Then the pilot raises a lever called the collective control. This tilts the spinning rotor blades so that they create more lift. As the pilot continues raising the collective control, the helicopter rises off the ground. To descend, the pilot lowers the collective control, flattening the rotor blades and reducing the lift produced by the rotor.

TO THE RESCUE!

Helicopters are the perfect aircraft for search and rescue operations on land or at sea. They can operate over any terrain, urban or rural, from sea level to high mountains. Helicopters can fly slowly while the crew scans the ground or water below for injured people, as seen in this search and rescue drill being performed in the San Francisco Bay. They can hover over one spot and are very useful for hoisting people from the sea or other inaccessible places if they need to be rescued.

STRAIGHT AHEAD

To make a helicopter fly forward, the pilot uses a control stick called the cyclic control. This tilts the main rotor forward. Greater lift is generated around the rear half of the rotor. This is because each blade is tilted as it goes around on its backward path but flattened again on its forward path. So each blade produces lots of lift when it is at the back, but much less lift when it reaches the front. This propels the helicopter forward.

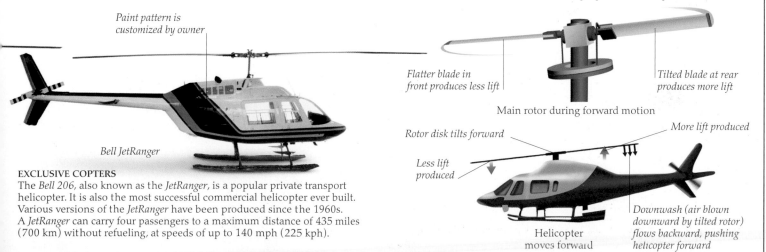

Paint pattern is customized by owner

Bell JetRanger

EXCLUSIVE COPTERS

The *Bell 206,* also known as the *JetRanger,* is a popular private transport helicopter. It is also the most successful commercial helicopter ever built. Various versions of the *JetRanger* have been produced since the 1960s. A *JetRanger* can carry four passengers to a maximum distance of 435 miles (700 km) without refueling, at speeds of up to 140 mph (225 kph).

Flatter blade in front produces less lift

Tilted blade at rear produces more lift

Main rotor during forward motion

Rotor disk tilts forward

More lift produced

Less lift produced

Downwash (air blown downward by tilted rotor) flows backward, pushing helicopter forward

Helicopter moves forward

Jet engines

IN THE 1930S, PROPELLER PLANES powered by piston engines were flying at speeds greater than 440 mph (700 kph), but the engines burned a lot of fuel. Jet engines helped airplanes achieve these speeds easily. The jet engine was invented in the late 1930s. The first jet-powered planes were military fighter jets. They entered service by the end of World War II as German and Allied forces looked to dominate the skies. After the war, aircraft manufacturers, such as Boeing and Douglas, built the first passenger jets. The superior power and speed of these aircraft made long-haul flights much shorter. Jet engines still power most modern military aircraft.

P-47 Thunderbolts in flight

BEFORE JETS
During World War II, the American propeller-driven *P-47 Thunderbolt* fighter was one of the fastest planes in the sky, reaching top speeds of more than 500 mph (800 kph). But engineers soon realized the limitations of propeller power. As propeller-driven aircraft approached the speed of sound—around 760 mph (1,225 kph)—the performance of their engines decreased and the planes became unstable. This speed limit that most planes could not cross was dubbed the "sound barrier." The jet engine was the key to breaking through the sound barrier.

Model of Hero's aeolipile

AEOLIPILE
In the 1st century CE, Greek scientist Hero of Alexandria described an engine called an aeolipile. This consisted of a boiler attached to a metal sphere, which spun around two pipes that held it in place. Heating the boiler turned water into steam, which passed into the sphere and out through two curved nozzles projecting from it. The escaping steam generated thrust, making the sphere spin. An aeolipile is a type of device called a reaction engine. It produces movement by expelling a jet of matter to produce thrust. The modern jet engine is a reaction engine too, so the aeolipile could be thought of as the first jet engine.

HOW IT WORKS
All jet engines work on the principle of Isaac Newton's third law of motion. It states that for every action, there is an equal and opposite reaction. Jet engines suck in air through the front, compress it, and then mix it with fuel in a combustion chamber. Igniting the fuel creates an explosion of hot gases that stream out of the rear of the engine, generating the thrust that pushes the plane forward. This engine is of type called a turbofan. The huge fan at the front of the engine not only pulls air through into the combustion chamber to burn the fuel. It also pulls a stream of cold air, called bypass air, around the engine and through the bypass duct, which produces extra thrust.

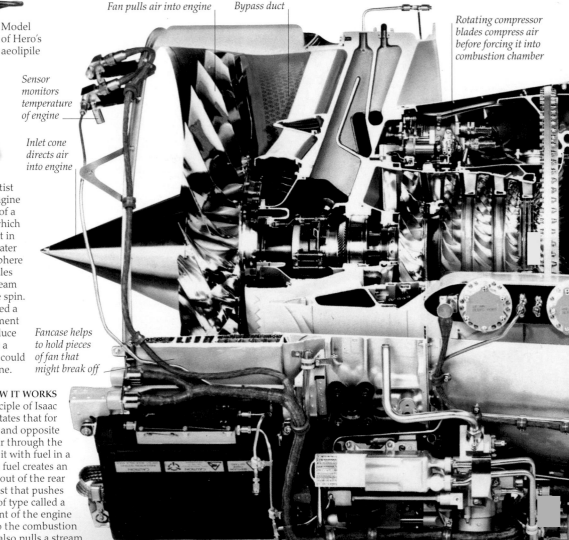

Fan pulls air into engine

Bypass duct

Rotating compressor blades compress air before forcing it into combustion chamber

Sensor monitors temperature of engine

Inlet cone directs air into engine

Fancase helps to hold pieces of fan that might break off

TURBO ENGINES

The three main types of jet engine are turbojets, turbofans, and turboprops. Turbojets are the simplest. Their hot exhaust gases pass through a turbine before streaming out at high speeds from the rear of the engine. In turn, the turbine drives a compressor that draws in more air through the engine. Some of the fastest aircraft use turbojets. Turboprops and turbofans are used by a variety of aircraft.

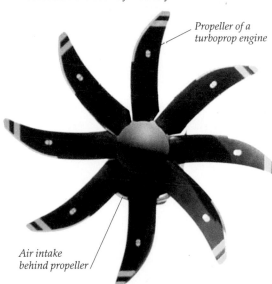

Propeller of a turboprop engine

Air intake behind propeller

THE FIRST JET ENGINE

British engineer and Royal Air Force officer Frank Whittle (shown on the right) designed the first jet engine in 1928, but took another nine years to build a working model—the Whittle Unit (WU) engine. Meanwhile, German engineer Hans von Ohain had designed and built his own jet engine. In 1939, it was used in the first jet-powered aircraft—the *Heinkel He 178*. The *Gloster E.28/39* was the first British aircraft to be powered by a jet engine—based on the WU. It made its maiden flight in 1941.

In a turboprop engine, the turbine (powered by the stream of hot gases from the combustion chamber) in turn powers a propeller at the front of the engine. It is the propeller alone that provides the forward thrust—not the stream of escaping exhaust gases. Turboprop engines power many small airliners as well as military transport planes of all sizes.

Combustion chamber is where fuel is ignited

Turbine is driven by exhaust gases, and its spinning motion powers fan and compressor

Heat shield prevents heat from exhaust gases from damaging turbine

Exhaust cone directs exhaust gases out of engine

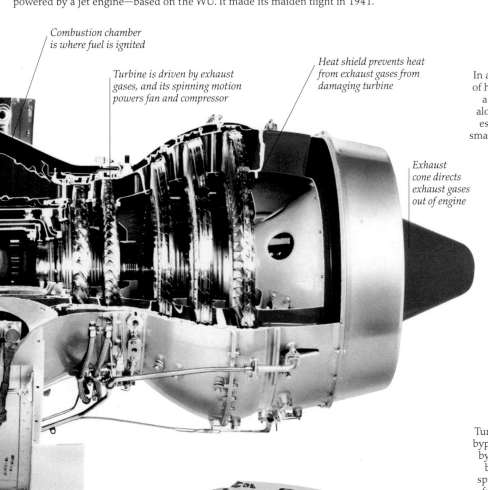

Titanium blade of fan

Turbofans are more efficient than other jet engines. In high bypass turbofans, most of the engine thrust comes from the bypass air. Most passenger jets use high bypass turbofans because these engines are more economical at cruising speeds. In low bypass turbofans, most of the thrust comes from the exhaust gases passing out of the engine. High-performance tactical fighters use low bypass turbofans, which sacrifice efficiency for an increase in speed.

COMMERCIAL JETLINERS

A collaboration between British and French aircraft manufacturers, *The Concorde* began ferrying passengers from London and Paris to New York in 1976. Its powerful turbojet engines reduced the time for transatlantic trips from 8 to 3.5 hours. In 2003, the aircraft was withdrawn from service because of its high flying costs and noisy engines. *The Concorde* was one of only two commercial passenger jets to fly faster than the speed of sound—the other was the Soviet *Tupolev Tu-144*.

The age of the car

THE AUTOMOBILE had a huge impact on society between the 1920s and 1960s—on the lives of the people as well as on the landscape. As cars became affordable, manufacturers expanded their range of models. They started to build simple family sedans, such as the Ford *Model Y*, as well as small city cars, both of which were aimed at middle-income families instead of wealthy buyers. As more people bought cars, traffic increased and new roads were built to ease the congestion. In 1956, the Interstate Highway System was authorized in the United States, making way for the first interconnected national highway system in the country.

Tailfin

Bullet-shaped taillight

NEED FOR SPEED
While some people could afford cheaper mass-produced cars in the 1930s, wealthy drivers were buying more expensive models—sports cars with powerful engines built for sheer speed. Car manufacturers such as Aston Martin, Bentley, and Bugatti tested out their new models in car races, such as Le Mans in France. Winning at these races was important because it made the cars more popular. Technologies born on the race track, such as the very powerful supercharged engines, were eventually added to the sports cars that ran on public roads.

Modern protective gear

Driver in a 1935 Aston Martin *Ulster* at a car race in 2009

ROAD NETWORKS
In the early days of driving, roads were often dirt tracks with stones and potholes that made driving dangerous and uncomfortable. Engineers and workers began improving road surfaces and expanding road networks. This enabled drivers to travel farther and in less traffic—these workers are laying tarmac to improve the road. In the US, the first stretch of the Interstate Highway network opened in Topeka, Kansas, in 1956. The network was completed 35 years later.

Road construction workers in the US, 1950s

STOP!
With the increase in traffic came traffic control measures, such as road signs, three-way traffic lights, speed limits, and traffic policemen. In Britain, roadside booths like this one were set up at junctions to help the policemen direct the flow of traffic. In the 1920s, automatic traffic signals began to replace the traffic booths. Many automatic signals started to be controlled by pressure pads in the road, which were triggered as the cars passed over them.

A LOVE AFFAIR
By the 1950s, most Americans aspired to owning a car and enjoying the freedom to travel that it provided. Even though the cost of a car was more than half the average family's annual income, more than 60 percent of American households owned a car. Suburbs were built in such a spaced-out way that cars became a necessity—to commute to work and go shopping—rather than a luxury. The mid-1950s to the mid-1960s was an era that spawned a car culture of drive-in movies, motels, and drive-through fast-food restaurants. The love affair with the automobile continues to the present day.

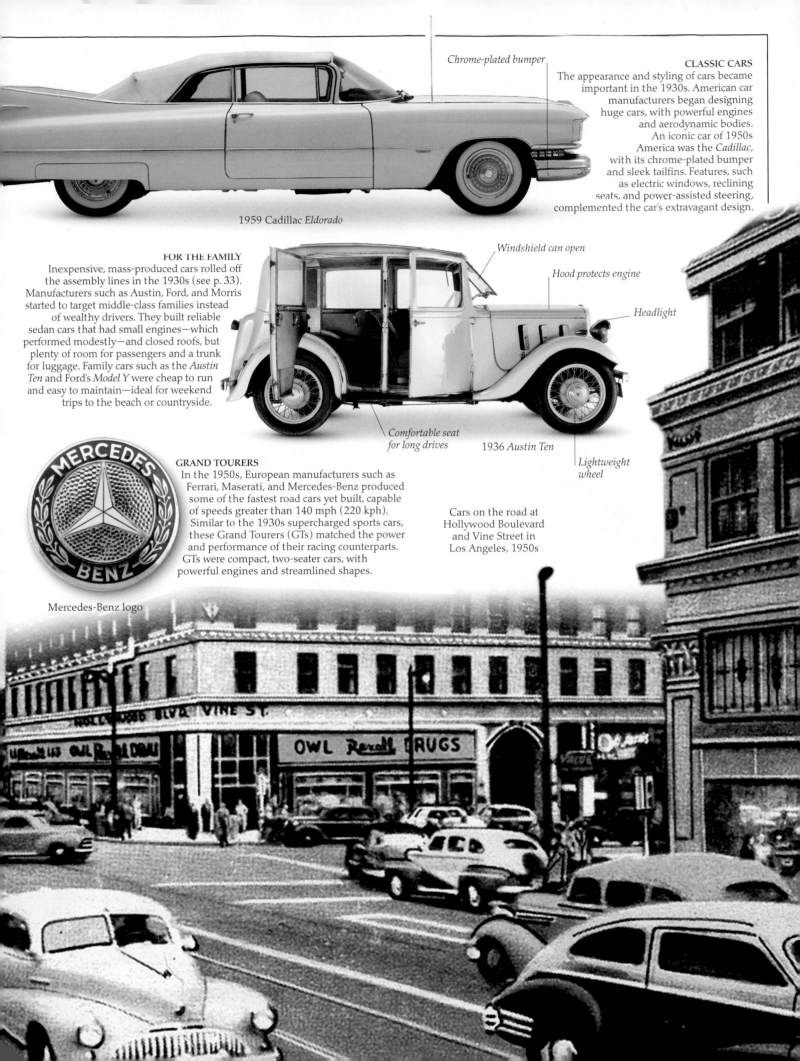

Chrome-plated bumper

CLASSIC CARS

The appearance and styling of cars became important in the 1930s. American car manufacturers began designing huge cars, with powerful engines and aerodynamic bodies. An iconic car of 1950s America was the *Cadillac*, with its chrome-plated bumper and sleek tailfins. Features, such as electric windows, reclining seats, and power-assisted steering, complemented the car's extravagant design.

1959 Cadillac *Eldorado*

FOR THE FAMILY

Inexpensive, mass-produced cars rolled off the assembly lines in the 1930s (see p. 33). Manufacturers such as Austin, Ford, and Morris started to target middle-class families instead of wealthy drivers. They built reliable sedan cars that had small engines—which performed modestly—and closed roofs, but plenty of room for passengers and a trunk for luggage. Family cars such as the *Austin Ten* and Ford's *Model Y* were cheap to run and easy to maintain—ideal for weekend trips to the beach or countryside.

Windshield can open

Hood protects engine

Headlight

Comfortable seat for long drives

1936 *Austin Ten*

Lightweight wheel

GRAND TOURERS

In the 1950s, European manufacturers such as Ferrari, Maserati, and Mercedes-Benz produced some of the fastest road cars yet built, capable of speeds greater than 140 mph (220 kph). Similar to the 1930s supercharged sports cars, these Grand Tourers (GTs) matched the power and performance of their racing counterparts. GTs were compact, two-seater cars, with powerful engines and streamlined shapes.

Cars on the road at Hollywood Boulevard and Vine Street in Los Angeles, 1950s

Mercedes-Benz logo

OWL *Rexall* DRUGS

Rockets

A ROCKET IS A TYPE OF JET ENGINE (see pp. 38–39) that propels objects at incredible speeds using the thrust produced by exhaust gases. However, unlike ordinary jet engines, rockets do not use oxygen from the air to burn fuel. Instead, they use a mixture of chemicals called propellants, which react explosively to generate thrust. Two types of propellant are used—a fuel and an oxidizer. The oxidizer is a chemical that produces the oxygen needed to burn the fuel. Rockets were first developed thousands of years ago in China. By the 13th century, the Chinese were fueling rockets with gunpowder. In the 20th century, rocket science developed rapidly, allowing spacecraft to be put in Earth orbit, land on the Moon, and explore space.

(see pp. 38–39)

LAUNCH SITES

This map shows many of the world's main spacecraft launch sites—they are found in every continent except Antarctica. Some sites, such as Cape Canaveral in Florida, are open to the public, while others are important military bases. Two sites are near the equator. The speed of Earth's rotation at the equator is around 1,040 mph (1,674 kph). This speed provides extra thrust to the rockets. Launch sites are kept well away from populated areas because of the possibility of falling debris in case of an explosion during a rocket's take off. This is also why sites are usually built near an ocean.

Equator

1. Edward, US
2. Wallops Island, US
3. Cape Canaveral, US
4. Kourou, French Guiana
5. Alcantara, Brazil
6. Plesetsk, Russia
7. Kapustin Yar, Russia
8. Palmachim, Israel
9. Baikonur, Russia
10. Sriharikota, India
11. Xichang, China
12. Taiyuan, China
13. Kagoshima, Japan
14. Tanegashima, Japan
15. Woomera, Australia

ROCKET SCIENCE

The working of a rocket follows Isaac Newton's third law of motion (see p. 38). The rocket pushes gas out (action) and the gas pushes back against the rocket (reaction). More reaction generates more thrust, which increases the rocket's speed. Rocket engines tend to work better in space than in Earth's atmosphere. In the atmosphere, the exhaust gases are slowed down by the air. Space is a vacuum (a region devoid of matter) so the exhaust gases are not slowed down.

(see p. 38)

Payload – a supply vehicle called Johannes Kepler sent to service the International Space Station (ISS)

Rocket nozzle of Ariane 5's upper stage boosts payload into orbit

Ariane 5 rocket with payload

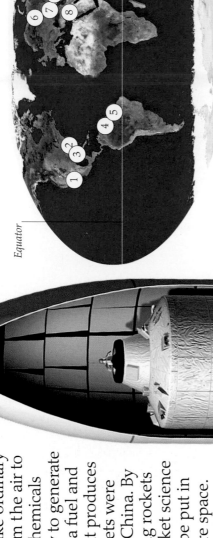

ROCKET PIONEERS

In the late 1800s, Russian mathematician Konstantin Tsiolkovsky worked out the thrust required for a rocket to escape Earth's gravity. He realised they could be used for space travel. Building on his work, American engineer Robert H. Goddard launched the first liquid-fuel rocket in 1926. Goddard's invention marked the beginning of modern rocketry—first as weapons, such as the German *V-2* and the nuclear missiles of several countries, and later for space exploration. Goddard is seen above, on the extreme left, checking a rocket's fuel pumps.

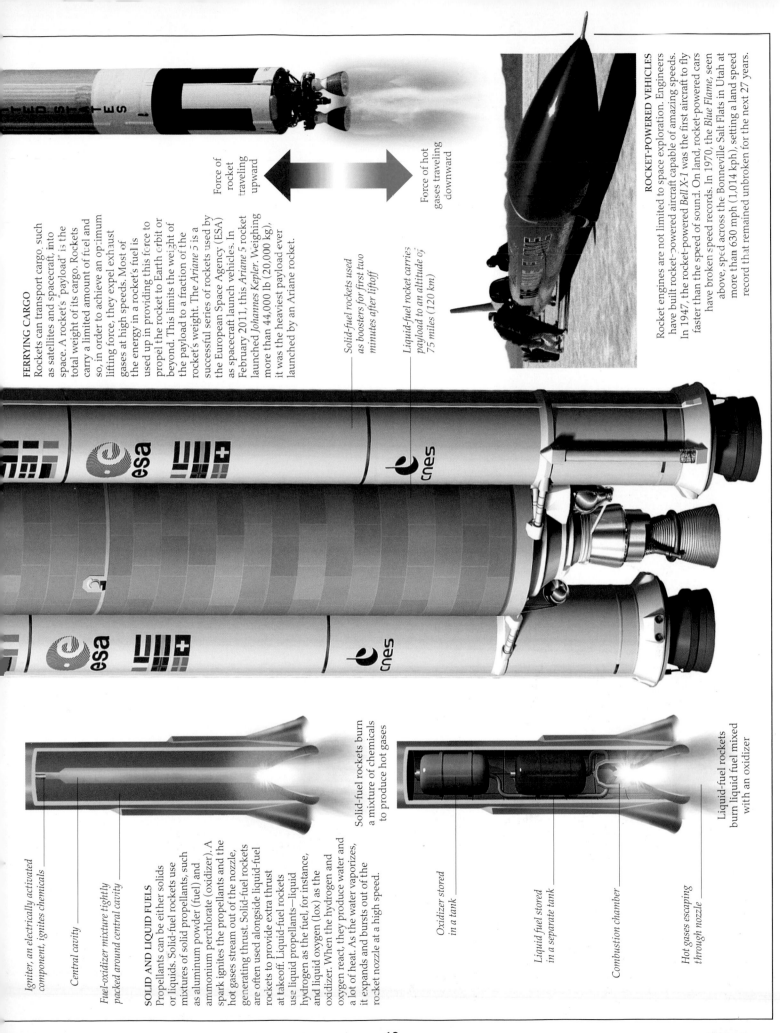

FERRYING CARGO

Rockets can transport cargo, such as satellites and spacecraft, into space. A rocket's "payload" is the total weight of its cargo. Rockets carry a limited amount of fuel and so, in order to achieve an optimum lifting force, they expel exhaust gases at high speeds. Most of the energy in a rocket's fuel is used up in providing this force to propel the rocket to Earth orbit or beyond. This limits the weight of the payload to a fraction of the rocket's weight. The *Ariane 5* is a successful series of rockets used by the European Space Agency (ESA) as spacecraft launch vehicles. In February 2011, this *Ariane 5* rocket launched *Johannes Kepler*. Weighing more than 44,000 lb (20,000 kg), it was the heaviest payload ever launched by an Ariane rocket.

Force of rocket traveling upward

Force of hot gases traveling downward

Solid-fuel rockets used as boosters for first two minutes after liftoff

Liquid-fuel rocket carries payload to an altitude of 75 miles (120 km)

SOLID AND LIQUID FUELS

Propellants can be either solids or liquids. Solid-fuel rockets use mixtures of solid propellants, such as aluminum powder (fuel) and ammonium perchlorate (oxidizer). A spark ignites the propellants and the hot gases stream out of the nozzle, generating thrust. Solid-fuel rockets are often used alongside liquid-fuel rockets to provide extra thrust at takeoff. Liquid-fuel rockets use liquid propellants—liquid hydrogen as the fuel, for instance, and liquid oxygen (lox) as the oxidizer. When the hydrogen and oxygen react, they produce water and a lot of heat. As the water vaporizes, it expands and bursts out of the rocket nozzle at a high speed.

Igniter, an electrically activated component, ignites chemicals

Central cavity

Fuel-oxidizer mixture tightly packed around central cavity

Solid-fuel rockets burn a mixture of chemicals to produce hot gases

Oxidizer stored in a tank

Liquid fuel stored in a separate tank

Combustion chamber

Hot gases escaping through nozzle

Liquid-fuel rockets burn liquid fuel mixed with an oxidizer

ROCKET-POWERED VEHICLES

Rocket engines are not limited to space exploration. Engineers have built rocket-powered aircraft capable of amazing speeds. In 1947, the rocket-powered *Bell X-1* was the first aircraft to fly faster than the speed of sound. On land, rocket-powered cars have broken speed records. In 1970, the *Blue Flame*, seen above, sped across the Bonneville Salt Flats in Utah at more than 630 mph (1,014 kph), setting a land speed record that remained unbroken for the next 27 years.

Journey to the Moon

A SPACE RACE BEGAN between the Soviet Union and the US in the late 1950s—each wanted to get ahead of the other in the field of space exploration. The Soviets scored a series of firsts—the first satellite in space and the first manned spaceflight. In 1961, President John F. Kennedy declared that sending a man to the Moon—and bringing him back safely—before the end of the decade was the primary goal of the American space program. The US spent billions of dollars on developing technology for a lunar landing. On July 20, 1969, the *Apollo 11* mission succeeded in landing American astronauts Neil Armstrong and Buzz Aldrin on the Moon, helping the US march ahead in the space race.

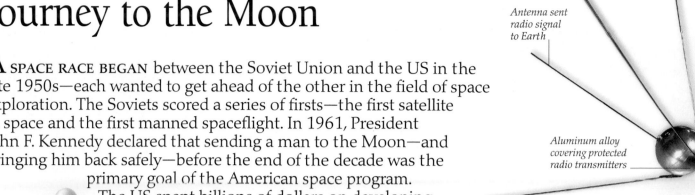

Antenna sent radio signal to Earth

Aluminum alloy covering protected radio transmitters

TAKING THE LEAD

On October 4, 1957, the Soviet Union launched *Sputnik 1* into Earth orbit. The first satellite in space, *Sputnik 1* circled Earth at more than 18,000 mph (27,000 kph). The satellite collected data about the upper atmosphere, beaming the results to Earth using radio signals. The data helped Soviet scientists prepare for the first manned space mission, which launched Soviet cosmonaut Yuri Gagarin into space in 1961. This let the Soviet Union take an early lead in the space race.

Command module

APOLLO SPACECRAFT

The National Aeronautics and Space Administration (NASA) developed the Apollo program—involving a series of Apollo spacecraft—to land a man on the Moon. During the 1960s, NASA conducted a number of spaceflights to prepare for the first lunar landing mission—*Apollo 11*. The *Apollo 11* spacecraft consisted of three parts, or modules—the Command Module (CM), Service Module (SM), and Lunar Module (LM). The CM was the control center for the long journey to and from the Moon. It was the only part of the Apollo spacecraft that returned to Earth intact. The SM housed the spacecraft's propulsion systems and power supply in the form of fuel cells and batteries. The LM was the lunar-landing module. It contained life-support systems and equipment for the astronauts to use on the Moon, as well as the engines for landing and takeoff.

Fuel tank

5. LM returns to lunar orbit to dock with CM and SM, which then fire the rocket to escape lunar orbit

4. LM lands on lunar surface

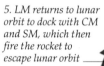

6. CM and SM return to Earth orbit

3. After LM separates for landing, CM and SM stay in lunar orbit with fuel for return to Earth

Service module

7. CM separates from SM and prepares to land on Earth

Antenna

Control console

2. CM and SM docked with LM transfer to lunar orbit

FLIGHT PLAN

NASA scientists devised a detailed flight plan for the *Apollo 11* mission—the Lunar Orbit Rendezvous (LOR). First, a giant *Saturn V* rocket launched the Apollo spacecraft with three astronauts on board into Earth orbit. Soon afterward, this rocket fired the spacecraft out of Earth orbit and on the 240,000-mile (390,000-km) journey to the Moon. Once in lunar orbit, two astronauts entered the LM to make the lunar landing, leaving one man behind in the CM in lunar orbit. After the astronauts finished their work on the Moon, the two parts of the spacecraft docked in lunar orbit, and the crew returned to Earth.

Lunar module, ascent stage (when taking off from the Moon)

Fuel tank

Equipment for experiments

Lunar Module descent stage (when landing on the Moon)

1. Saturn V rocket launches Apollo 11 into Earth orbit

Landing pad

ROCKETING INTO SPACE

The *Saturn V* rocket used to launch each Apollo spacecraft into space is the most powerful launch vehicle ever built. Each of these rockets stood 363 ft (110 m) tall and weighed 3,000 tons (2,700 metric tons) when fully loaded with fuel. *Saturn V* was a three-stage liquid-fuel rocket. The first stage fired for 2.5 minutes, taking the spacecraft to a height of 37.5 miles (60 km) and a speed of nearly 6,000 mph (10,000 kph). The second stage fired for nearly six minutes, accelerating the spacecraft into Earth orbit at a speed of more than 15,500 mph (25,000 kph). The final stage fired twice—first to maintain the spacecraft in Earth orbit and then again to propel it toward the Moon.

US flag

Saturn V rocket about to launch at Cape Canaveral, Florida

Thrusters control direction of spacecraft's movement

Service arms supply rocket with fuel and power before launch

THE EAGLE HAS LANDED

On July 20, 1969, Neil Armstrong and Edwin "Buzz" Aldrin landed the LM, nicknamed *Eagle*, on an area of the Moon called the Sea of Tranquillity. Live television images watched by almost 600 million people across the world showed the two astronauts stepping on to the lunar surface. Armstrong and Aldrin spent 2.5 hours on the Moon, collecting rock and soil samples, taking photographs, and performing experiments. Then they fired up the *Eagle's* ascent engine, rejoined the CM carrying Michael Collins, and started the 71-hour voyage back to Earth.

Buzz Aldrin on the Moon

US Navy divers collect the Apollo 11 astronauts in a life raft

SPLASHDOWN

On July 24, 1969, the *Apollo 11* astronauts embarked on one of the most dangerous parts of the mission—the return to Earth. As the CM reentered our atmosphere, drag (see p. 34) caused its heat shield to heat up to a scorching 5,000°F (2,760°C). This disrupted Mission Control's radio contact with the incoming spacecraft. Minutes later, Neil Armstrong's voice crackled over the radio. The three astronauts had safely splashed down 825 miles (1,330 km) west of Hawaii in the Pacific Ocean.

THE APOLLO PROGRAM

The *Apollo 11* mission was the high point of the Apollo program, but it wasn't the end of lunar exploration. NASA launched another six missions to the Moon. Five Apollo missions were successful, landing 10 more astronauts on the lunar surface. One mission, *Apollo 13*, was aborted when a fuel tank ruptured, although the astronauts safely returned to Earth. More missions were planned, but rising costs led to the termination of the Apollo program in 1972.

Insignia of the Apollo 12, Apollo 16, and Apollo 17 missions

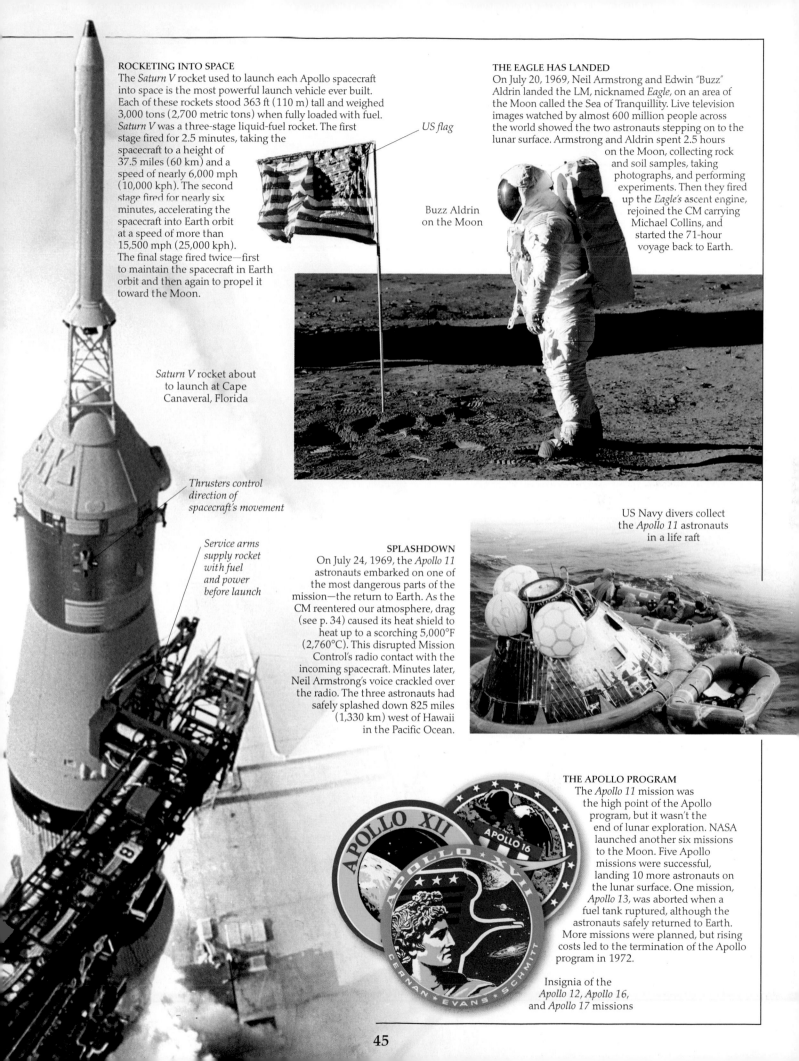

Exploring space

Capsule
carries three
astronauts

Johannes Kepler,
a supply vehicle,
docked at ISS

HUMANS BEGAN TO EXPLORE SPACE in the second half of the 20th century, when scientists designed powerful rockets that could transport spacecraft into Earth orbit and beyond. Today, more than 10 countries regularly launch vehicles into space, from communications satellites to unmanned space probes. Manned vehicles, such as the Russian *Soyuz* spacecraft and NASA's recently retired space shuttles, act as space "taxis," ferrying astronauts and supplies on missions to the International Space Station (ISS)—an orbiting scientific research platform that is permanently crewed. Unmanned probes have visited every planet in our solar system—from the early flybys of Mars and Venus by the *Mariner* probes to the *Cassini-Huygens* probe that studied Saturn and its moons. The data gleaned by these probes are helping space scientists plan future manned missions to other planets in our solar system and search for signs of life beyond Earth.

SHUTTLES IN SPACE
NASA built five operational shuttles as part of its Space Transport System (STS)—*Discovery, Atlantis, Endeavour, Columbia,* and *Challenger,* although the last two were destroyed in tragic accidents. NASA's space shuttle fleet entered service in 1981 and the spacecraft have flown on 135 missions to launch satellites, space probes, and equipment, such as the Hubble Space Telescope, as well as for carrying astronauts to and from the ISS. *Atlantis* was the last shuttle to fly and NASA retired the fleet in 2011. The space shuttle was—and still is—the only reusable spacecraft.

LAUNCHING INTO SPACE
A *Soyuz* rocket lifts off from Baikonur Cosmodrome, Kazakhstan, carrying three Russian cosmonauts (Russian astronauts) to the ISS. The *Soyuz* spacecraft is the oldest human spaceflight system in active service and has been ferrying cosmonauts and cargo into space since 1967. Following the retirement of NASA's space shuttle fleet in 2011, *Soyuz* is the only way to transport astronauts to the ISS. The ISS also keeps a docked *Soyuz* capsule as an escape craft for the crew in case of an emergency.

Solar panel
array generates
power for lander

Ramp opened up on Pathfinder
lander to deploy Sojourner *rover*

SPACEWALK!

On June 3, 1965, astronaut Edward H. White II, the pilot of NASA's *Gemini 4* spacecraft, became the first American to step outside his spacecraft and "walk" in the microgravity ("weightlessness") of Earth orbit. His spacewalk, or extra-vehicular activity (EVA), lasted 23 minutes. During an EVA, astronauts wear multilayered spacesuits and portable life-support systems to supply them with air and water, and protect them from the harsh environment of space. Today, astronauts commonly carry out EVAs to perform tasks, such as maintenance work on sections of the ISS.

Handheld maneuvering unit controls direction of movement of astronaut

Tether and umbilical connects astronaut to spacecraft

Communications array

CSM

Space shuttle Endeavour docked with ISS

Main thruster

THE FUTURE OF SPACEFLIGHT

NASA commissioned the *Orion* spacecraft in 2006 to replace the aging space shuttle fleet, and to conduct future manned missions to the Moon and, eventually, to Mars and the other planets in the solar system. *Orion*'s design is based on the successful *Apollo* configuration, with a crew and service module (CSM) to hold a crew of four to six astronauts. The design also incorporates some of the technologies from the space shuttles, such as improved waste-management systems. *Orion* is due to replace NASA's shuttle fleet in 2016.

Solar panel

OUT IN THE UNKNOWN

This panoramic view of the Martian landscape was taken by the Mars *Pathfinder* lander. The Mars *Pathfinder* spacecraft, carrying the *So___* rover, was launched on December 4, 1996, and reached M___ uly 4, 1997. *Pathfinder* sent a lander to the Martian surface, from which the rover emerged. Space probes have been used to explore all the planets in the solar system, and have even travele___ nd. *Voyager 2* flew past Neptune in 1989 and has since ____ed out of the solar system. It continues to beam data about the Sun's magnetic field back to scientists on Earth.

EXPLORING MARS

The six-wheeled *Sojourner* rover was equipped with laser "eyes" to navigate on the Martian surface and avoid obstacles along the way. *Sojourner* spent more than two months on Mars, conducting experiments to study the planet's atmosphere, climate, and geology, sending a lot of data back to NASA—including 550 images of the Martian landscape.

Small world

AIRPLANES POWERED BY JET ENGINES have revolutionized air travel since the mid-20th century. The era of jet airliners really took off in the 1950s with the Douglas *DC-8* and the Boeing *707*—they were large enough to 200 or more many passengers and cruised at up to 600 mph (1,000 kph), crossing oceans in a few hours. At this time, flying on passenger jets was available only to wealthy passengers and was relatively rare. In the 1970s, a generation of wide-bodied airliners, including the massive Boeing *747* "jumbo jet," took to the skies and soon made air travel affordable for more people. In Europe and the US, many families began flying to foreign countries for their vacations instead of visiting local destinations. The world seems much smaller than it did 50 years ago.

A SHRINKING WORLD
The golden age of jet travel dawned in 1970, when American manufacturer Boeing introduced the Boeing *747*. The plane built on the success of one of its predecessors—the Boeing *707*—offering more seats and shorter journey times between many destinations around the world. As competition between airliners increased, low-cost airlines emerged as a cheaper alternative. Skytrain, run by British entrepreneur Sir Freddie Laker (seen above), was one such airline. For the first time, ordinary people began traveling by air, boosting tourism, trade, and businesses.

BEFORE THE JET AGE
In the early days of air travel, airlines promoted air travel as a speedier but equally luxurious alternative to ocean liners. The US was the leader in world aviation, with airlines such as Pan American (Pan Am) and TWA locked in a fierce battle to attract customers to the skies. Only wealthy people—movie stars, sports celebrities, and businesspeople—could afford to fly in those days.

1946 poster advertising
Pan Am flights to Bermuda

SUPERJUMBO

In 2007, the Airbus *A380* superjumbo entered service as the largest passenger jet in the world. Almost 40 years after the *747* started flying, the Airbus *A380* is its first real challenger in the very large airliner market. This huge aircraft is roughly the same length as a Boeing *747*, at 239 ft (72.7 m) long, but it has 50 percent more cabin space. This is because it is the world's first fully double-decker airliner, with an upper deck stretching along its entire length. This gives room for up to 853 passengers. Its engines are also more efficient, burning 20 percent less fuel per passenger than the *747*.

Airbus *A380*

Rolls Royce Trent 900 turbofan engine, one of four that power the airplane

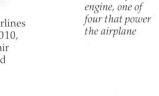

FLYING ACROSS THE WORLD

This map shows 56,749 routes used by 669 airlines between 3,310 airports across the world. In 2010, around 629.5 million passengers traveled by air within the US, and 91 million passengers used US-based airlines to travel to international destinations. The world's busiest airports include Hartsfield-Jackson in Atlanta and Heathrow in London, which have more than 65 million passengers passing through their terminals every year.

AT THE AIRPORT

This aerial photograph shows one of the terminals at Charles de Gaulle Airport, outside Paris, France. Airports have grown from small military airstrips into major international hubs that handle millions of passengers every year. A modern airport is divided into landside and airside areas. The landside area caters to passengers and includes parking lots, bus and rail links, check-in counters, stores and restaurants, passport and security control centers, passenger lounges, and boarding gates. The airside area caters to aircraft and includes runways, taxiways, docking bays, fueling facilities, maintenance hangars, air-traffic control, and emergency services.

PRIVATE JETS

While Boeing was developing planes for the masses, other aircraft manufacturers such as Cessna, Learjet, and Gulfstream were building smaller private jets for business use and affluent travelers. Since the late 1960s, private jets have become the ultimate status symbol, allowing the superrich and famous to travel when and where they want. Private jets are built for comfort and elegance, as shown by this image of the cabin of a *G5 Executive Gulfstream* jet.

CONTROLLING TRAFFIC

Air-traffic controllers in this control tower are directing aircraft as they move around an airport. A controller must keep all the planes a certain distance apart, both on the ground and in the air. The controller must also decide the order of aircraft taking off from the runway and landing on it. Controllers stay in touch with pilots by radio and monitor all the aircraft in their zone using radar screens. Each aircraft flying near the airport appears as a dot on the screen. The radar helps determine the distance of the aircraft from the airport as well as its altitude.

Ships of today

WATERCRAFT HAVE BECOME increasingly specialized and are now specifically built for many different purposes, such as transporting cargo and leisure activities. Today's sea cargo may be transported loose. Ships called bulk carriers carry grain and mineral ores, among other items, while tankers transport liquid cargo, such as oil and liquefied gas. Nearly everything else is "containerized," and is shipped in standard metal boxes usually 20 ft (6.1 m) or 40 ft (12.2 m) long. These containers form a global transportation system along with standard container-port machinery. Passenger ships have been largely replaced by catamarans and hydrofoils over short distances, and by airliners over longer distances. Cruise ships, however, remain popular, as do jet-skis and powerboats.

Containers stacked on deck

SUPERTANKERS
Oil tankers are specialized cargo ships that transport crude oil and refined petroleum products to and from oilfields and refineries around the world. Between the 1950s and 1970s, oil tankers changed from 22,000-ton (20,000-metric-ton) vessels to massive supertankers, such as the *Seawise Giant*, which was launched in 1979 and could carry 600,000 tons (550,000 metric tons) of crude oil. During the "supertanker era" of 1973–1979, conflict between Israel and Egypt meant that the Suez Canal—a vital waterway for commercial ships—was closed to traffic. Meanwhile, bigger supertankers continued to be made because they could transport oil more cheaply. Since the Suez Canal reopened, however, these supertankers have become less useful, because they can't fit through the canal and have to travel around Africa.

SHIPPING CARGO
Despite advances in air travel, shipping cargo over the seas remains the cheapest way of transporting cargo between different continents. Container ships have highly efficient, supercharged diesel engines and crews of fewer than 10 people, making the ships a cost-effective option for shifting cargo. Most container ships can carry between 1,000 and 2,000 containers. The largest cargo vessels—such as Maersk's E-class of ultra-large container vessels (ULCVs)—carry around 11,000 containers on every trip.

Thick metal cable called hawser is used for towing

CMA CGM CARTAGENA
MONROVIA
IMO 9122033

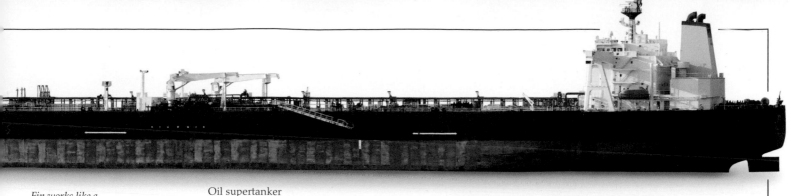

Oil supertanker

Fin works like a wing with the aerofoil shape creating lift

Propeller drives vessel forward

Hull rises out of water when boat moves at a high speed

IN PORT

Different ports handle different types of ship, from small ports that service fishing vessels to large cruise ship ports such as the Port of Miami. Most cargo ports are bulk ports, which means they handle many different types of cargo, from grain and valuable ores to cars and liquid chemicals. Cranes can be seen here loading containers onto a ship docked at the Port of Singapore—one of the world's busiest cargo ports. Containers that arrive on vessels are handled by the container-port machinery, which seamlessly loads them directly onto trains or trucks to reach their final destination.

MOVING ON FINS

Hydrofoils are high-speed boats that ride on winglike fins mounted beneath the hull. At low speeds, the hydrofoil moves like any other boat, with the hull dragging through the water. At higher speeds, water moves faster over the top surface of the fins than the bottom surface. This reduces water pressure above the fins, producing a lift force that pushes the entire hull out of the water. There is much less drag and the boat moves even faster.

JETS OF WATER

Jet-skis are watercraft used mainly for fun. Here, former world champion Masao Fujisawa performs an acrobatic stunt on his jet-ski. Jet-skis work by jet propulsion, using a type of propeller called an impeller. This sucks water through an inlet at the bottom of the craft and pushes it out as a high-speed jet at the rear. Swiveling the water jet provides the force for moving the jet-ski in different directions. The impeller is concealed in the body of the jet-ski, so these vessels can be used in shallow coastal waters, where normal propeller blades might break off.

GUARDING THE COAST

The United States Coast Guard (USCG) is responsible for the security of the coastal waters of the US and the safety of vessels moving in these waters. The USCG operates a fleet of small boats and larger vessels called cutters. The small boat fleet patrols inland waterways and coastal waters. It includes powerboats carrying medical equipment and high-speed interceptor boats. Cutters are more than 65 ft (20 m) long and include coastal patrol vessels and search-and-rescue ships.

US Coast Guard emblem

High bridge, or wheelhouse, provides clear line of sight

NEED A TUG?

A tugboat tows a giant container ship into the port of Barcelona in Spain. Tugboats are small vessels that help maneuver larger ships through narrow canals or crowded harbors, or pull vessels that cannot move themselves, such as disabled ships and oil platforms. Tugboats may be small but they have powerful engines—usually run by diesel—and hydraulic towing machinery. The engines are often the same as those used to power railroad locomotives and provide up to 27,000 horsepower (hp)—roughly equal to 225 average family cars.

MONTBRIO

High-speed trains

WHEN THE FIRST HIGH-SPEED TRAIN SERVICE opened in Japan in 1964, it cut the journey time between Tokyo and Osaka from 6.5 to 4 hours. Today's high-speed trains are even faster and make the same journey in just over 2 hours. Many other countries have followed Japan's example and built their own high-speed rail networks—such as France's TGV network and China's CRH network. The world's fastest passenger trains regularly travel at more than 155 mph (250 kph). They are so fast that they compete with jet aircraft for passengers.

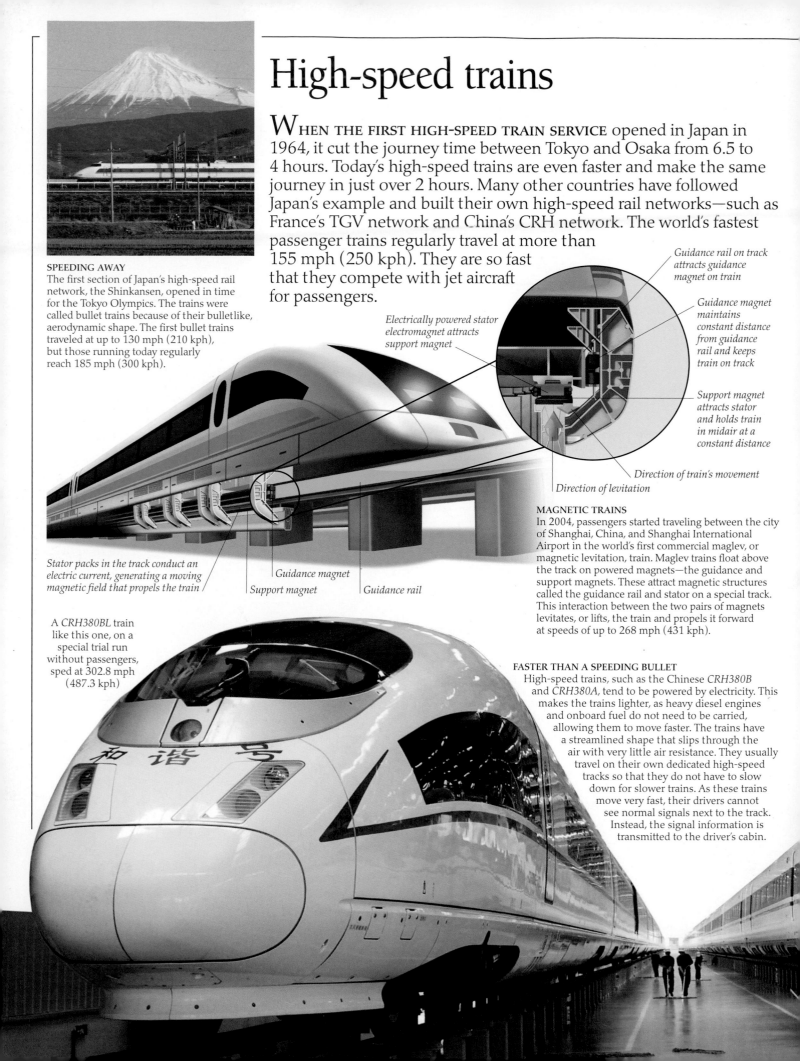

SPEEDING AWAY
The first section of Japan's high-speed rail network, the Shinkansen, opened in time for the Tokyo Olympics. The trains were called bullet trains because of their bulletlike, aerodynamic shape. The first bullet trains traveled at up to 130 mph (210 kph), but those running today regularly reach 185 mph (300 kph).

Guidance rail on track attracts guidance magnet on train

Guidance magnet maintains constant distance from guidance rail and keeps train on track

Electrically powered stator electromagnet attracts support magnet

Support magnet attracts stator and holds train in midair at a constant distance

Direction of train's movement

Direction of levitation

Stator packs in the track conduct an electric current, generating a moving magnetic field that propels the train

Guidance magnet

Support magnet

Guidance rail

A *CRH380BL* train like this one, on a special trial run without passengers, sped at 302.8 mph (487.3 kph)

MAGNETIC TRAINS
In 2004, passengers started traveling between the city of Shanghai, China, and Shanghai International Airport in the world's first commercial maglev, or magnetic levitation, train. Maglev trains float above the track on powered magnets—the guidance and support magnets. These attract magnetic structures called the guidance rail and stator on a special track. This interaction between the two pairs of magnets levitates, or lifts, the train and propels it forward at speeds of up to 268 mph (431 kph).

FASTER THAN A SPEEDING BULLET
High-speed trains, such as the Chinese *CRH380B* and *CRH380A*, tend to be powered by electricity. This makes the trains lighter, as heavy diesel engines and onboard fuel do not need to be carried, allowing them to move faster. The trains have a streamlined shape that slips through the air with very little air resistance. They usually travel on their own dedicated high-speed tracks so that they do not have to slow down for slower trains. As these trains move very fast, their drivers cannot see normal signals next to the track. Instead, the signal information is transmitted to the driver's cabin.

STRAIGHT THROUGH

Most high-speed trains need tracks without sharp bends, because these would slow them down. This becomes a problem in mountainous terrain. Engineers generally solve this problem by building tracks that go straight through the mountains. The Gotthard Base Tunnel is a 35-mile- (57-km-) long tunnel being dug through the Swiss Alps by giant tunnel boring machines—the machine seen here is called "Heidi." When the tunnel opens in 2016, it will be the world's longest rail tunnel. Trains will go through it at speeds of up to 155 mph (250 kph).

ONE TICKET, MANY COUNTRIES

The high-speed trains in Europe are built to specifications or standards that are common across the European countries. This allows the trains to move easily from one country to the next. A passenger's ticket may, therefore, cover travel in multiple countries. Eurostar trains, for example, run from England through the Channel Tunnel to France and Belgium. Their international terminals resemble airports, with customs and immigration facilities.

Ticket

TILTING TRAINS

When a high-speed train turns through a bend, passengers experience a sideways force that can be uncomfortable and makes things slide around. One way to make passengers more comfortable as high-speed trains round corners is to make them tilt. The most successful tilting trains in service today are the Italian Pendolino trains. As a Pendolino goes into a bend, built-in systems called hydraulic actuators tilt it by eight degrees. This slight tilt increases cornering speeds by about 20 percent.

A *CRH380A* train like this one, on a special trial run without passengers, recorded a top speed of 302 mph (486.1 kph)

Modern motoring

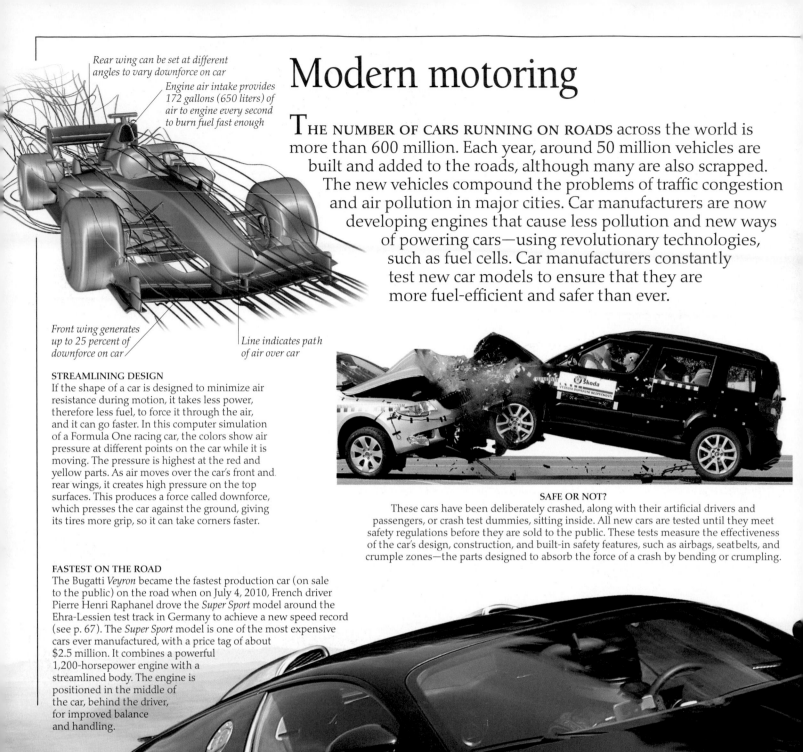

Rear wing can be set at different angles to vary downforce on car

Engine air intake provides 172 gallons (650 liters) of air to engine every second to burn fuel fast enough

Front wing generates up to 25 percent of downforce on car

Line indicates path of air over car

THE NUMBER OF CARS RUNNING ON ROADS across the world is more than 600 million. Each year, around 50 million vehicles are built and added to the roads, although many are also scrapped. The new vehicles compound the problems of traffic congestion and air pollution in major cities. Car manufacturers are now developing engines that cause less pollution and new ways of powering cars—using revolutionary technologies, such as fuel cells. Car manufacturers constantly test new car models to ensure that they are more fuel-efficient and safer than ever.

STREAMLINING DESIGN

If the shape of a car is designed to minimize air resistance during motion, it takes less power, therefore less fuel, to force it through the air, and it can go faster. In this computer simulation of a Formula One racing car, the colors show air pressure at different points on the car while it is moving. The pressure is highest at the red and yellow parts. As air moves over the car's front and rear wings, it creates high pressure on the top surfaces. This produces a force called downforce, which presses the car against the ground, giving its tires more grip, so it can take corners faster.

FASTEST ON THE ROAD

The Bugatti *Veyron* became the fastest production car (on sale to the public) on the road when on July 4, 2010, French driver Pierre Henri Raphanel drove the *Super Sport* model around the Ehra-Lessien test track in Germany to achieve a new speed record (see p. 67). The *Super Sport* model is one of the most expensive cars ever manufactured, with a price tag of about $2.5 million. It combines a powerful 1,200-horsepower engine with a streamlined body. The engine is positioned in the middle of the car, behind the driver, for improved balance and handling.

SAFE OR NOT?

These cars have been deliberately crashed, along with their artificial drivers and passengers, or crash test dummies, sitting inside. All new cars are tested until they meet safety regulations before they are sold to the public. These tests measure the effectiveness of the car's design, construction, and built-in safety features, such as airbags, seatbelts, and crumple zones—the parts designed to absorb the force of a crash by bending or crumpling.

TRAVELING ROUGH

Sport Utility Vehicles (SUVs) are designed to cope with off-road driving on rough terrain. In most cars, only the two front wheels are connected to the engine, while the rear ones just roll along as the cars move. In an SUV, all four wheels are turned by the engine. This arrangement gives the wheels the maximum grip on slippery, loose, or soft surfaces. This SUV is taking part in the Barcelona–Dakar rally—an off-road race across the Sahara Desert.

Car contains fuel cell

Hydrogen fueling station uses solar energy to make hydrogen fuel from water

Internal combustion engine

RUNNING ON HYDROGEN

Most cars are powered by engines that burn fuel made from oil (petroleum). However, the diminishing oil supply and the pollution caused by burning have spurred the development of new ways for powering vehicles. One such technology is the fuel cell. This produces electricity by means of a chemical reaction between hydrogen fuel and oxygen from the air. The electricity then powers an electric car's motor. The toy car shown above is the *H-Racer*, which is powered by a hydrogen fuel cell.

HYBRIDS

Hybrid electric vehicles (HEVs) have an internal combustion engine (see pp. 28–29) and one or more electric motors. The Toyota *Prius* was the world's first mass-produced HEV. It is normally powered by an electric motor. The gasoline engine automatically takes over if the motor's battery is running low or if the driver needs to go faster than the electric motor. While it runs, the gasoline engine also charges the battery.

Low, streamlined body

Engine of Toyota *Prius*

Electric motor

COMPUTERS AND CARS

Most modern cars contain multiple computers. One of these controls the Satellite Navigation (SatNav) by using GPS (the Global Positioning System). Its GPS receiver uses a network of satellites to pinpoint the vehicle's location. This information is then illustrated on a map, allowing the user to navigate to the destination. Another computer controls the instruments and displays that provide information about fuel levels and speed. Yet another system, called the Engine Control Unit (ECU), monitors the engine to ensure that it is working at maximum efficiency.

Bugatti *Veyron* 16.4 roadster

Display of GPS navigation system

Fun on wheels

SOME VEHICLES USED TODAY for leisure actually started out as utility vehicles—vehicles designed for specific tasks. An example is the modern quad bike, which was developed in the 1970s for use in farming and forestry, but eventually began to be used for trail riding and racing. Other vehicles used for fun are conventional vehicles that have been specially modified. Hot rods, for example, are ordinary cars given a makeover with a more powerful engine and a remodeled body. There are still other vehicles that are designed specifically for fun, such as ultralight aircraft, which were created in the 1970s to make flying more affordable.

Manual control to adjust speed

SKATING ON ELECTRICITY
This skateboard is powered by an electric motor. The motor is connected to the wheels and allows the skateboard to cover a distance of 12–19 miles (20–30 km) at a top speed of 25 mph (40 kph). The motor also makes it possible for a user to cruise uphill. A skateboarder steers the skateboard by shifting his or her weight in one direction, and changes the speed with a manual control.

RUNNING EVERYWHERE
All-terrain vehicles (ATVs), also known as quad bikes, are great for riding on all kinds of off-road surfaces, from deserts and beaches to muddy fields. These four-wheeled motorcycles are widely used by farmers to move around on their land. They can tow trailers carrying animal food, tools, or supplies, but they are also used for trail riding and competition sports. Some are built specially for cross-country, desert, and mud racing.

BALANCING ACT
This Segway electric vehicle is moving on two wheels and, amazingly, it can balance itself. Computers in its base control motors that drive its wheels. Sensors detect whether the vehicle is tilting and automatically turn the wheels to bring it upright. Its speed and direction change when the rider shifts his or her weight. Segways are used for transportation by some businesses and police forces. In some places, tourists use them for sightseeing. Despite having a top speed of only 12.5 mph (20 kph), the Segway has also spawned new sports. Here, Apple Computers founder Steve Wozniak is playing in the Segway polo world championship.

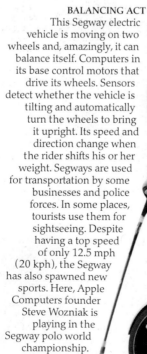

Tires can be as large as 66 in (1.7 m) in diameter

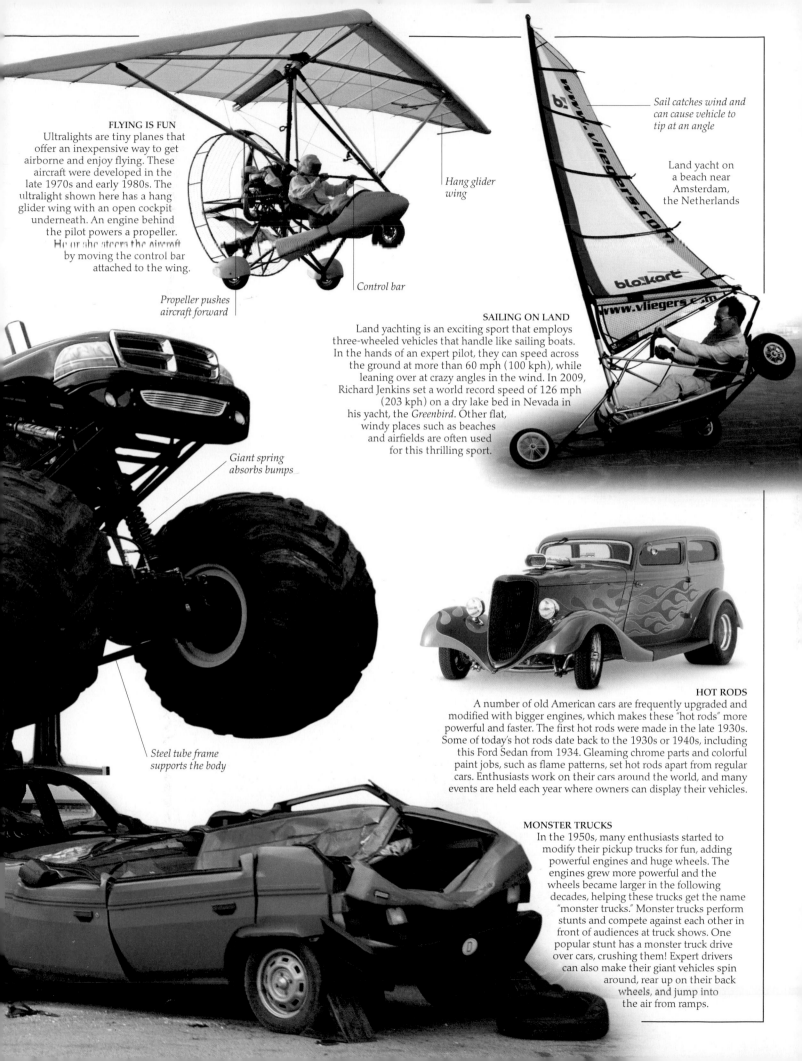

FLYING IS FUN
Ultralights are tiny planes that offer an inexpensive way to get airborne and enjoy flying. These aircraft were developed in the late 1970s and early 1980s. The ultralight shown here has a hang glider wing with an open cockpit underneath. An engine behind the pilot powers a propeller. He or she steers the aircraft by moving the control bar attached to the wing.

Hang glider wing

Control bar

Propeller pushes aircraft forward

Sail catches wind and can cause vehicle to tip at an angle

Land yacht on a beach near Amsterdam, the Netherlands

SAILING ON LAND
Land yachting is an exciting sport that employs three-wheeled vehicles that handle like sailing boats. In the hands of an expert pilot, they can speed across the ground at more than 60 mph (100 kph), while leaning over at crazy angles in the wind. In 2009, Richard Jenkins set a world record speed of 126 mph (203 kph) on a dry lake bed in Nevada in his yacht, the *Greenbird*. Other flat, windy places such as beaches and airfields are often used for this thrilling sport.

Giant spring absorbs bumps

Steel tube frame supports the body

HOT RODS
A number of old American cars are frequently upgraded and modified with bigger engines, which makes these "hot rods" more powerful and faster. The first hot rods were made in the late 1930s. Some of today's hot rods date back to the 1930s or 1940s, including this Ford Sedan from 1934. Gleaming chrome parts and colorful paint jobs, such as flame patterns, set hot rods apart from regular cars. Enthusiasts work on their cars around the world, and many events are held each year where owners can display their vehicles.

MONSTER TRUCKS
In the 1950s, many enthusiasts started to modify their pickup trucks for fun, adding powerful engines and huge wheels. The engines grew more powerful and the wheels became larger in the following decades, helping these trucks get the name "monster trucks." Monster trucks perform stunts and compete against each other in front of audiences at truck shows. One popular stunt has a monster truck drive over cars, crushing them! Expert drivers can also make their giant vehicles spin around, rear up on their back wheels, and jump into the air from ramps.

The *F/A-18E Super Hornet* is a bigger and advanced version of the *F/A-18 Hornet* (see bottom right). The US Navy began using the *Super Hornet* in 1999.

War machines

MODERN WARFARE is highly mechanized, and almost every type of vehicle has been adapted for military use. Tanks were developed during World War I, as were the first military planes. Within 50 years, these propeller-driven, wooden aircraft evolved into supersonic (faster than sound) fighters, and in less than 100 years, into bombers that can fly into enemy territory without being detected. Today's military aircraft range from super-heavy cargo planes, which transport troops, tanks, and even folding bridges into war zones, to tiny unmanned spy planes. However, the biggest war machines today are the immense aircraft carriers sailing the seas.

The *F-22A Raptor* is a supersonic stealth fighter. Its shape is designed to stop radar waves from being reflected straight back to the enemy radar systems. This makes the plane less visible to enemy radar.

Gun turret can swivel

Armored Humvee

HUMVEES
This High Mobility Multipurpose Wheeled Vehicle (HMMWV), or Humvee, is an example of a small, lightly armored vehicle designed to protect the driver and passengers from small-arms fire and shrapnel (fragments of exploding bombs and artillery shells). The light weight and small size makes the Humvee faster and more maneuverable than bigger and more heavily armored vehicles, such as tanks. Lightly armored vehicles transport people and cargo. They are usually unarmed, but if required, they may be equipped with a weapon, such as a machine gun.

FAST ATTACKS
Fighter aircraft are small, fast, highly maneuverable planes designed for combat with enemy aircraft. Some fighters are designed to fly one particular type of mission. For instance, interceptors are fighters that prevent enemy aircraft from reaching their targets, while air superiority fighters take control of an enemy's air space. Fighters that can fly various types of mission are called multirole combat aircraft. Stealth fighters are designed using shapes and materials that make it hard for enemy radars and heat-seeking missiles to detect them. Most fighters have radar that monitors the air-space around the planes, searching for and tracking threats such as enemy aircraft.

Gun fires large shells

Turret can move through 360 degrees

ARMED AND ARMORED
Tanks are heavily armored fighting vehicles with a large gun mounted in a rotating turret. A tank can weigh more than 65 tons (60 metric tons). Modern tanks, such as this US Army *M1/A1 Abrams*, have computer-controlled firing systems. A laser rangefinder measures the distance to a target. A computer then calculates where to aim the gun, taking into account the weather conditions and even the bending effect of gravity on the gun's barrel.

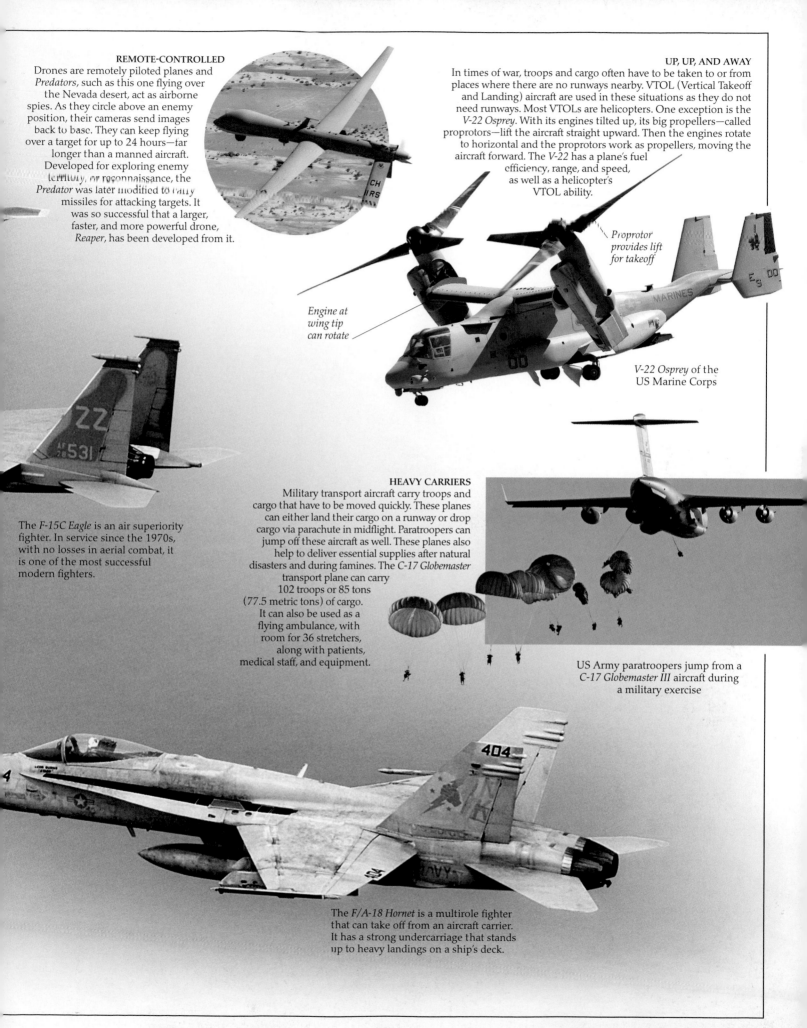

REMOTE-CONTROLLED
Drones are remotely piloted planes and *Predators*, such as this one flying over the Nevada desert, act as airborne spies. As they circle above an enemy position, their cameras send images back to base. They can keep flying over a target for up to 24 hours—far longer than a manned aircraft. Developed for exploring enemy territory, or reconnaissance, the *Predator* was later modified to carry missiles for attacking targets. It was so successful that a larger, faster, and more powerful drone, *Reaper*, has been developed from it.

UP, UP, AND AWAY
In times of war, troops and cargo often have to be taken to or from places where there are no runways nearby. VTOL (Vertical Takeoff and Landing) aircraft are used in these situations as they do not need runways. Most VTOLs are helicopters. One exception is the *V-22 Osprey*. With its engines tilted up, its big propellers—called proprotors—lift the aircraft straight upward. Then the engines rotate to horizontal and the proprotors work as propellers, moving the aircraft forward. The V-22 has a plane's fuel efficiency, range, and speed, as well as a helicopter's VTOL ability.

Proprotor provides lift for takeoff

Engine at wing tip can rotate

V-22 Osprey of the US Marine Corps

The *F-15C Eagle* is an air superiority fighter. In service since the 1970s, with no losses in aerial combat, it is one of the most successful modern fighters.

HEAVY CARRIERS
Military transport aircraft carry troops and cargo that have to be moved quickly. These planes can either land their cargo on a runway or drop cargo via parachute in midflight. Paratroopers can jump off these aircraft as well. These planes also help to deliver essential supplies after natural disasters and during famines. The *C-17 Globemaster* transport plane can carry 102 troops or 85 tons (77.5 metric tons) of cargo. It can also be used as a flying ambulance, with room for 36 stretchers, along with patients, medical staff, and equipment.

US Army paratroopers jump from a *C-17 Globemaster* III aircraft during a military exercise

The *F/A-18 Hornet* is a multirole fighter that can take off from an aircraft carrier. It has a strong undercarriage that stands up to heavy landings on a ship's deck.

Running on a reactor

A NEW POWER SOURCE WAS INTRODUCED to transportation in 1956. It was nuclear power—the energy locked up in the center of an atom. It drove the submarine *USS Nautilus* for a record 1,381 miles (2,222 km) in 90 hours, entirely under water. So much power is contained in nuclear fuel that nuclear vessels carry enough to keep going for years. And unlike coal- and oil-driven engines, nuclear reactors need no air to burn their fuel, so they provide an ideal way to power submarines under water. Previously, most submarines, when submerged, ran their diesel engines on compressed air from tanks or used electric motors. They were successful weapons in World Wars I and II, but they had to surface to take on more air or charge their batteries with diesel engines. Today, nuclear reactors are used mainly in submarines and giant military ships.

NUCLEAR ENERGY
This uranium-rich fuel rod is glowing in the reactor core of a nuclear power plant. Uranium is a radioactive substance, which means its atoms are very unstable. During nuclear fission, these unstable atoms split into two smaller, more stable atoms—usually of the elements barium and krypton. The splitting releases nuclear energy in the form of light—bright blue in this case—and heat. This energy heats water, converting it into steam, which drives a turbine. Radioactive uranium is dangerous to human health, so a thick shield surrounds the reactor on a submarine or aircraft carrier to protect the crew.

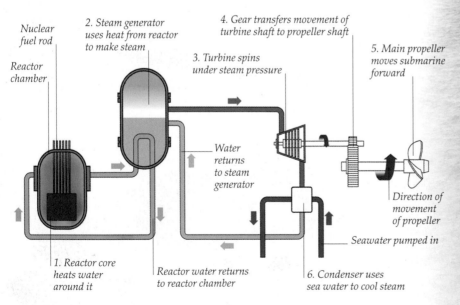

Nuclear fuel rod

Reactor chamber

2. Steam generator uses heat from reactor to make steam

3. Turbine spins under steam pressure

4. Gear transfers movement of turbine shaft to propeller shaft

5. Main propeller moves submarine forward

Water returns to steam generator

Direction of movement of propeller

Seawater pumped in

1. Reactor core heats water around it

Reactor water returns to reactor chamber

6. Condenser uses sea water to cool steam

NUCLEAR PROPULSION
The engines of all modern nuclear-powered vessels are based on the design of the reactor used to power the *USS Nautilus*, above. Inside the reactor core, nuclear fission splits atoms of radioactive uranium, releasing a lot of energy. This heats water that turns into steam. The pressure of the steam drives the main turbine, which is linked to the propeller by a geared propeller shaft. Some of the steam is diverted through a smaller turbine, which generates electricity for other systems on the submarine.

USS George Washington, a nuclear-powered aircraft carrier

JUGGERNAUT

Two nuclear reactors power this 100,000-ton juggernaut—the Nimitz-class aircraft carrier *USS George Washington*—allowing it to cover 200,000 miles (360,000 km) without the need to refuel. The ship carries about 6,000 crew members; 85 aircraft, including fighter jets, helicopters, and service planes; and a huge payload of bombs, guided missiles, rockets, and torpedoes. This makes it one of the strongest warships at sea.

UNDERWATER FLEET

The 350-ft- (107-m-) long *USS Connecticut*, seen above, is one of three Seawolf-class, fast-attack submarines in active duty for the US Navy. Since nuclear power fuels this vessel and supplies the crew with oxygen, it can remain submerged for months at a time, hidden from enemy ships. Powered by a single reactor, this vessel is designed to track and destroy enemy ships and is armed with missiles and torpedoes. The US navy has the largest fleet of nuclear submarines in the world. Some are fast-attack submarines, but others are designed to launch long-range ballistic missiles.

LIVING AT SEA

A typical nuclear submarine has a crew of more than 100 sailors, who live and work in cramped conditions for up to six months at a time. New technologies have been developed to allow crews to work comfortably. The atmosphere inside a submarine is controlled by machines that add oxygen and remove carbon dioxide and other waste gases from the air. Other machines purify sea water for the reactor and for drinking, cleaning, and cooking. Sea water is used directly to flush toilets.

A sailor irons his uniform in the submarine *USS Annapolis*

A NUCLEAR DREAM

In the 1950s, scientists were still realizing the full potential of nuclear power. The Ford Motor Company came up with the concept of a nuclear-powered car—the Ford *Nucleon*. Instead of a gasoline engine, it would run on steam power produced by a nuclear reactor in the rear of the car. The design suggested that the car would run for 5,000 miles (8,000 km) before replacing the nuclear fuel. The Ford Motor Company built a half-scale model, but the car never progressed further due to fears about the safety of nuclear power and the possibility of a disastrous meltdown.

William Ford with a model of the *Nucleon*

Future of transportation

FIFTY YEARS AGO, flying cars, jetpacks, and space travel for ordinary people were seen as the future of transportation—ideas like these seemed fantastical at the time. Today, all three have become reality in a small way. Commercial space travel companies have already started to offer the public the chance to fly into Earth orbit. Tomorrow's technologies might even enable manned missions to other planets. Back on Earth, our dependence on oil—a daily global usage of around 3.6 billion gallons (14 billion liters)—will cause supplies to run out by 2050, according to some estimates. Vehicles of the future will rely on new fuels and technologies.

WhiteKnightTwo has two hulls

FLYING INTO THE FUTURE

As technology advances, vehicles and craft will continue to evolve. By 2050, aircraft manufacturer Airbus aims to make flying a truly interactive experience. Passenger airliners would use biometric scanning to check the identity of passengers using unique physical or behavioral characteristics. The airliner seats would swivel and adapt to fit different body shapes. Once airborne, the cabin wall will become see-through at the touch of a button, offering passengers sweeping, panoramic views of everything around the plane.

PERSONAL RAPID TRANSPORTATION

As the number of cars on the roads continues to increase, it will become more necessary than ever to rely on public transportation to get around. A potential example might be a Personal Rapid Transit (PRT) system, such as the Urban Light Transit (ULTra). PRT systems are designed to carry between one and six passengers in small electric vehicles known as podcars, which run along dedicated guideways. These podcars are running on the 2.4-mile- (3.9-km-) long ULTra PRT system that serves London's Heathrow Airport, connecting the terminals with the airport's parking lots. Each pod carries up to four passengers per trip and is powered by an energy-efficient battery pack.

DRIVERLESS CARS

In 2010, American car manufacturer General Motors unveiled its vision for the future of driving—the EN-V (Electric Networked Vehicle). This two-wheeled, battery-powered car is designed for busy city centers. Once charged, the EN-V will have a top speed of 25 mph (40 kph) and a range of about 25 miles (40 km).

One amazing feature of the EN-V is that it will be driverless. It will move automatically, using wireless technology to communicate with other EN-Vs on the road. Sensors will help the vehicle keep a safe distance from others on the road, and park safely.

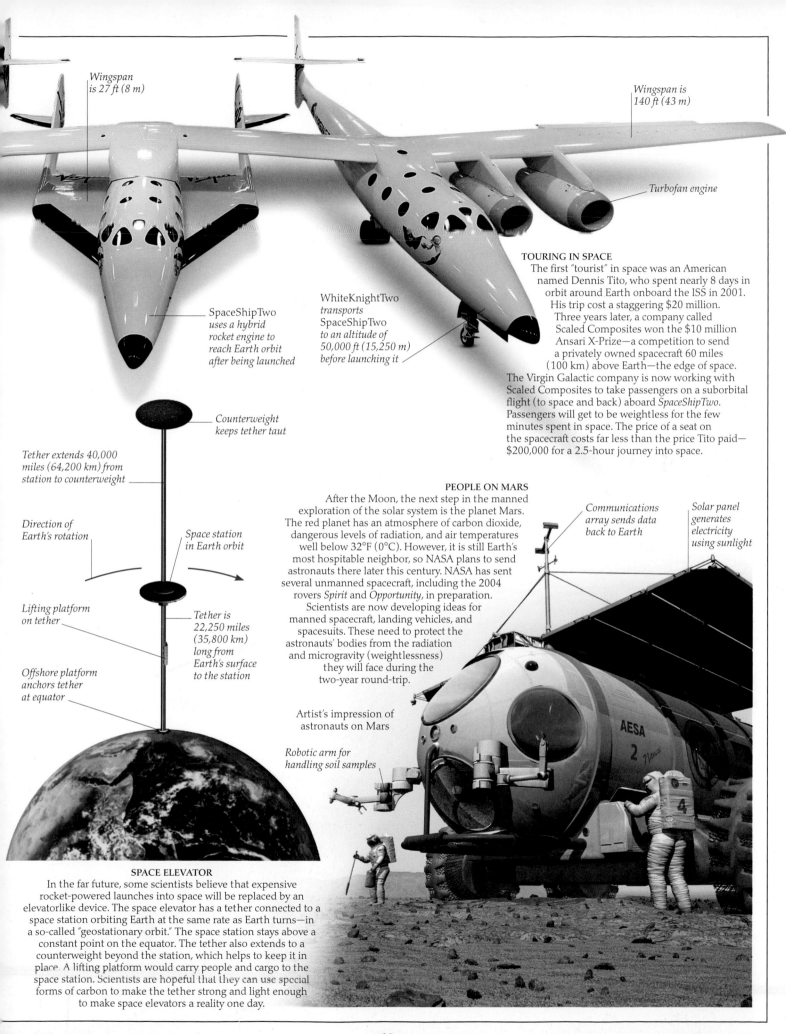

Wingspan is 27 ft (8 m)

Wingspan is 140 ft (43 m)

Turbofan engine

SpaceShipTwo uses a hybrid rocket engine to reach Earth orbit after being launched

WhiteKnightTwo transports SpaceShipTwo to an altitude of 50,000 ft (15,250 m) before launching it

TOURING IN SPACE

The first "tourist" in space was an American named Dennis Tito, who spent nearly 8 days in orbit around Earth onboard the ISS in 2001. His trip cost a staggering $20 million. Three years later, a company called Scaled Composites won the $10 million Ansari X-Prize—a competition to send a privately owned spacecraft 60 miles (100 km) above Earth—the edge of space. The Virgin Galactic company is now working with Scaled Composites to take passengers on a suborbital flight (to space and back) aboard *SpaceShipTwo*. Passengers will get to be weightless for the few minutes spent in space. The price of a seat on the spacecraft costs far less than the price Tito paid—$200,000 for a 2.5-hour journey into space.

Counterweight keeps tether taut

Tether extends 40,000 miles (64,200 km) from station to counterweight

Direction of Earth's rotation

Space station in Earth orbit

Lifting platform on tether

Tether is 22,250 miles (35,800 km) long from Earth's surface to the station

Offshore platform anchors tether at equator

PEOPLE ON MARS

After the Moon, the next step in the manned exploration of the solar system is the planet Mars. The red planet has an atmosphere of carbon dioxide, dangerous levels of radiation, and air temperatures well below 32°F (0°C). However, it is still Earth's most hospitable neighbor, so NASA plans to send astronauts there later this century. NASA has sent several unmanned spacecraft, including the 2004 rovers *Spirit* and *Opportunity*, in preparation. Scientists are now developing ideas for manned spacecraft, landing vehicles, and spacesuits. These need to protect the astronauts' bodies from the radiation and microgravity (weightlessness) they will face during the two-year round-trip.

Communications array sends data back to Earth

Solar panel generates electricity using sunlight

Artist's impression of astronauts on Mars

Robotic arm for handling soil samples

SPACE ELEVATOR

In the far future, some scientists believe that expensive rocket-powered launches into space will be replaced by an elevatorlike device. The space elevator has a tether connected to a space station orbiting Earth at the same rate as Earth turns—in a so-called "geostationary orbit." The space station stays above a constant point on the equator. The tether also extends to a counterweight beyond the station, which helps to keep it in place. A lifting platform would carry people and cargo to the space station. Scientists are hopeful that they can use special forms of carbon to make the tether strong and light enough to make space elevators a reality one day.

Timelines

MOTORIZED TRANSPORTATION on land and sea and in the air has changed the world so much in the last 100 years. It is easy to forget that for the great majority of history, transportation amounted horse-drawn vehicles and wind-driven boats. Wheeled vehicles are 30 times older than motorized transportation, since they were developed by the ancient Mesopotamians as early as 3500 BCE. Most transportation innovation has happened since the Industrial Revolution in the 18th and 19th centuries. In fact, steam engines and internal combustion engines are key inventions that have helped spark industrial and technological progress.

Water

Humans started using rafts and other simple vessels perhaps as early as 50,000 BCE. Ships with sails were developed much later, around 3500 BCE. Today, engines power ships across the seas.

1492 COLUMBUS
Italian sailor Christopher Columbus lands in the Bahamas off North America—around 500 years after Viking sailors reached the continent.

1521 MAGELLAN
Portuguese explorer Ferdinand Magellan leads the first expedition to to circumnavigate the globe, but dies near the Philippines.

Ferdinand Magellan

1450   1500   1550   1600

Land

After the wheel, the advent of the steam engine was the next big milestone in the history of transportation. Many other major developments took place from the 18th century onward.

1829 RAINHILL TRIALS
Father and son George and Robert Stephenson build a steam locomotive called *Rocket* that wins the Rainhill Trials.

Illustration of *Rocket*

1869 GOLDEN SPIKE
Railroad workers lay the ceremonial final spike of the world's first transcontinental railroad at Promontory Summit, Utah, to link the East and West coasts of the US.

1769 CUGNOT TRACTOR
French engineer Nicolas-Joseph Cugnot builds the first steam-powered car, a tractorlike vehicle called the *fardier à vapeur* (steam dray).

Cugnot tractor

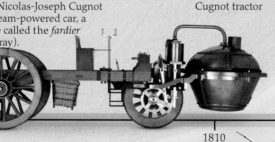

1846 PNEUMATIC TIRE
Scottish inventor Robert William Thomson invents the pneumatic tire, 43 years before John Boyd Dunlop makes it a commercial success.

1852 SAFETY ELEVATOR
Elisha Otis develops the safety elevator and exhibits it two years later at the New York World's Fair.

1760   1810   1835   1860   1885

Air and space

Major developments in air and space travel have taken place since the beginning of the 20th century, starting with the pioneering work of the Wright brothers.

1920 AUTOGYRO
Spanish engineer Juan de la Cierva develops the autogyro—the forerunner of the helicopter.

1947 BELL-X1
Rocket-powered aircraft *Bell X1*, piloted by American Chuck Yeager, flies faster than the speed of sound.

Bell X-1

1903 FLYER 1
American brothers Orville and Wilbur Wright pioneer powered, controlled flight on the *Flyer 1* at Kitty Hawk.

Flyer 1

1926 GODDARD
American physicist Robert Goddard launches the first liquid-fuel rocket, nicknamed Nell.

1932 AMELIA EARHART
American aviator Amelia Earhart becomes the first woman to fly solo across the Atlantic Ocean.

1900   1910   1920   1930   1940

Model of *Turtle*

1807 STEAMBOATS
American engineer Robert Fulton launches the *Clermont,* one of the first successful steamboats, which sails along the Hudson River between New York City and Albany.

Medal commemorating *USS Nautilus*

1955 NUCLEAR SUBS
The US Navy launches *USS Nautilus*—the first nuclear-powered submarine.

1953 TRIESTE LAUNCHES
Seven years later, in 1960, this submersible makes the deepest manned dive in history, reaching the bottom of a trench in the Pacific Ocean.

Container ship carrying cargo

1775 TURTLE
American inventor David Bushnell builds the *Turtle,* the first submarine used in combat.

1838 ATLANTIC CROSSING
The *Great Western* becomes the first steamship to make regular Atlantic crossings.

1866 TRANSATLANTIC CABLE
The *Great Eastern* lays the first telecommunications cable to cross the Atlantic.

1966 CONTAINER SHIPS
The Moore-McCormack company starts the first transatlantic container service.

1650 1700 1800 1850 1900 1950 2000

1908 MODEL T
American inventor Henry T. Ford employs mass-production techniques to build the Ford *Model T.*

1964 HIGH-SPEED TRAINS
The *Tokaido Shinkansen* high-speed railroad opens between Tokyo and Osaka in Japan. High-speed trains begin running around the world in the following years.

2010 SUPER SPORT
Bugatti *Veyron Super Sport* reaches a speed of 268 mph (431 kph), the fastest achieved by any production car.

Ford *Model T,* 1909–1910

Bugatti *Veyron Super Sport*

1910 1960 1985 2010

Yuri Gagarin

1986 MIR
Russian space station *Mir* begins operating in Earth orbit. It remains there until 2001.

2011 SHUTTLE PROGRAM ENDS
On July 21, the space shuttle *Atlantis* touches down after its final mission, marking the end of the space shuttle program.

Endeavour launch

1961 FIRST MAN IN SPACE
Soviet cosmonaut Yuri Gagarin becomes the first person in space, completing one orbit around Earth in *Vostok 1.*

1969 MAN ON MOON
American astronauts Neil Armstrong and Buzz Aldrin become the first people to set foot on the Moon during the successful *Apollo 11* mission.

1998 ISS
Space agencies from Canada, Europe, Japan, Russia, and the US start building the International Space Station (ISS).

1960 1970 1980 1990 2000 2010

Speedsters

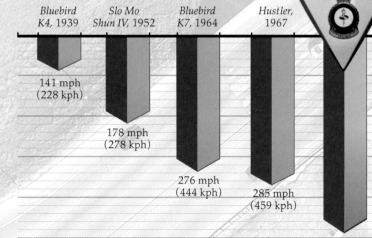

Spirit of Australia

THE HISTORY OF TRANSPORTATION is dotted with cases of intense rivalry between vehicles—cars, planes, ships, or trains—in their bid to become the fastest in their class. Scientists and engineers have worked tirelessly to build vehicles that achieve the best aerodynamics and the maximum power. Drivers and pilots have, meanwhile, risked their lives driving these speed machines to their absolute limits. Listed here are some of the world speed records in air, and on land and water.

Running on rails

On April 3, 2007, a French TGV (*Train à Grande Vitesse*) *V150* locomotive set the world record for the fastest train running on wheels. It reached a speed of 357 mph (574.8 kph) on a section of high-speed track between Paris and Strasbourg, France. The train did not carry passengers and had been specially modified to set the record.

TGV V150, 2007, 357 mph (575 kph)

TGV Atlantique, 1990, 320 mph (515 kph)

ICE-V, 1988, 253 mph (406 kph)

Class 962 Shinkansen, 1979, 198 mph (319 kph)

Class 1000 Shinkansen, 1964, 159 mph (256 kph)

RAIL RECORDS
This diagram shows the top speeds achieved by conventional trains running on wheels. However, experimental sleds and maglev vehicles can be even faster. The fastest-ever speed for a manned vehicle running on rails was achieved by a rocket sled driven by John Stapp, in 1954. The vehicle traveled at more than 600 mph (1,000 kph) on a track at Holloman Air Force Base in the US. In 2003, an experimental Japanese JR-Maglev train set a record of 361 mph (581 kph) on a magnetic-levitation track (see p.52) in Yamanashi, Japan.

On water

The official water speed record was set by the jet-powered hydroplane *Spirit of Australia*. Ken Warby piloted it to a speed of 317 mph (511 kph) at Blowering Dam in New South Wales, Australia, on 8 October 1978. This vessel now rests at the Australian National Maritime Museum. The *Union Internationale Motonautique* (UIM) governs speed records set by waterborne vehicles.

Bluebird K4, 1939 — 141 mph (228 kph)

Slo Mo Shun IV, 1952 — 178 mph (278 kph)

Bluebird K7, 1964 — 276 mph (444 kph)

Hustler, 1967 — 285 mph (459 kph)

317 mph (511 kph)

WATER RECORDS
This diagram shows world water speed records over time. Father and son Malcolm and Donald Campbell achieved a string of successes in their *Bluebird* vessels in the 1930s and 1960s, respectively.

TGV V150

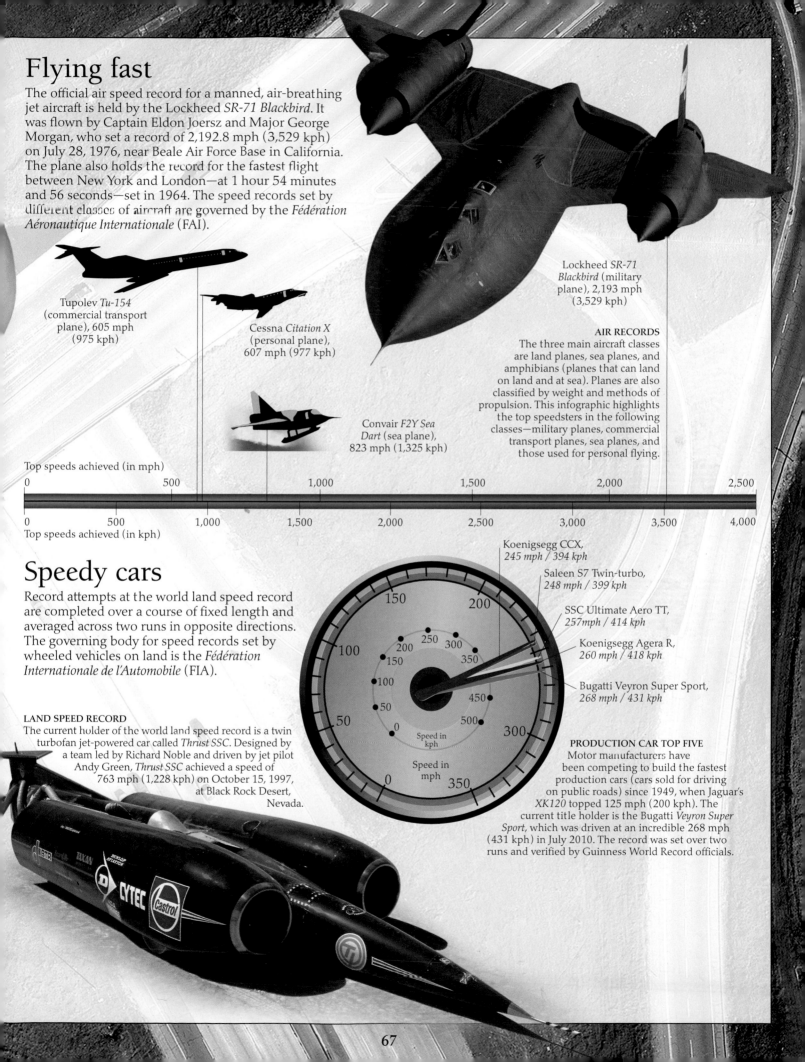

Flying fast

The official air speed record for a manned, air-breathing jet aircraft is held by the Lockheed *SR-71 Blackbird*. It was flown by Captain Eldon Joersz and Major George Morgan, who set a record of 2,192.8 mph (3,529 kph) on July 28, 1976, near Beale Air Force Base in California. The plane also holds the record for the fastest flight between New York and London—at 1 hour 54 minutes and 56 seconds—set in 1964. The speed records set by different classes of aircraft are governed by the *Fédération Aéronautique Internationale* (FAI).

Tupolev *Tu-154*
(commercial transport plane), 605 mph
(975 kph)

Cessna *Citation X*
(personal plane),
607 mph (977 kph)

Convair *F2Y Sea Dart* (sea plane),
823 mph (1,325 kph)

Lockheed *SR-71 Blackbird* (military plane), 2,193 mph
(3,529 kph)

AIR RECORDS
The three main aircraft classes are land planes, sea planes, and amphibians (planes that can land on land and at sea). Planes are also classified by weight and methods of propulsion. This infographic highlights the top speedsters in the following classes—military planes, commercial transport planes, sea planes, and those used for personal flying.

Top speeds achieved (in mph)

| 0 | 500 | 1,000 | 1,500 | 2,000 | 2,500 |

| 0 | 500 | 1,000 | 1,500 | 2,000 | 2,500 | 3,000 | 3,500 | 4,000 |

Top speeds achieved (in kph)

Speedy cars

Record attempts at the world land speed record are completed over a course of fixed length and averaged across two runs in opposite directions. The governing body for speed records set by wheeled vehicles on land is the *Fédération Internationale de l'Automobile* (FIA).

LAND SPEED RECORD
The current holder of the world land speed record is a twin turbofan jet-powered car called *Thrust SSC*. Designed by a team led by Richard Noble and driven by jet pilot Andy Green, *Thrust SSC* achieved a speed of 763 mph (1,228 kph) on October 15, 1997, at Black Rock Desert, Nevada.

Koenigsegg CCX,
245 mph / 394 kph

Saleen S7 Twin-turbo,
248 mph / 399 kph

SSC Ultimate Aero TT,
257mph / 414 kph

Koenigsegg Agera R,
260 mph / 418 kph

Bugatti Veyron Super Sport,
268 mph / 431 kph

Speed in kph

Speed in mph

PRODUCTION CAR TOP FIVE
Motor manufacturers have been competing to build the fastest production cars (cars sold for driving on public roads) since 1949, when Jaguar's *XK120* topped 125 mph (200 kph). The current title holder is the Bugatti *Veyron Super Sport*, which was driven at an incredible 268 mph (431 kph) in July 2010. The record was set over two runs and verified by Guinness World Record officials.

Record breakers

In the short history of motorized transportation, many scientists and engineers have been driven to develop record-breaking vehicles, either for the challenge of breaking the record itself, or to advance transportation technology in general. As inventors strive to improve their designs and make transport more efficient, many records will continue to be broken. One record that will stand forever, though, is the deepest dive by a submersible. In 1960, *Trieste* dived as deep as it is possible to dive when it reached the bottom of the world's oceans.

FERRARI F1 TEAM

Most successful car-racing team	
• Years active	1950–2011
• Constructors' championships	16
• Drivers' championships	15

The Scuderia Ferrari is the only team to have competed in every Formula 1 season since 1950. The *F-150* (above) competed in 2011.

ECLIPSE

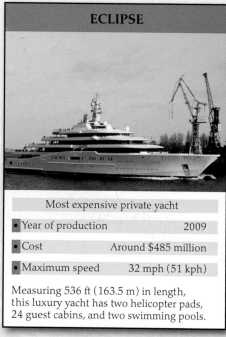

Most expensive private yacht	
• Year of production	2009
• Cost	Around $485 million
• Maximum speed	32 mph (51 kph)

Measuring 536 ft (163.5 m) in length, this luxury yacht has two helicopter pads, 24 guest cabins, and two swimming pools.

EMMA MÆRSK

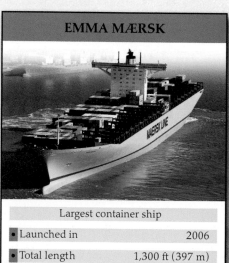

Largest container ship	
• Launched in	2006
• Total length	1,300 ft (397 m)
• Maximum power	109,000 horsepower

The *Emma Mærsk* and each ship in its class has a maximum speed of 29 mph (47 kph) and can carry up to 15,000 containers.

NS 50 LET POBEDY

Largest icebreaker (ice-clearing ship)	
• Launched in	2007
• Total length	522 ft (159 m)
• Maximum power	75,000 horsepower

Powered by twin nuclear reactors, this ship can break through ice up to 8 ft (2.5 m) thick on expeditions through the Arctic Ocean.

GRAF ZEPPELIN

First airship to cross the Atlantic Ocean	
• First flew in	1928
• Maximum speed	80 mph (128 kph)
• Maximum power	2,650 horsepower

In its 9 years of service, this airship made 590 flights and covered more than 1 million miles (1.6 million km).

AIRBUS A380

Largest passenger airplane	
• First flight	2005
• Total length	239 ft (72.7 m)
• Maximum speed	587 mph (945 kph)

The Airbus *A380* can fly 853 passengers from New York to Hong Kong nonstop.

B-52 STRATOFORTRESS

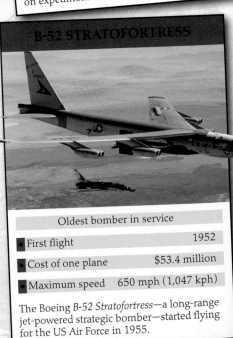

Oldest bomber in service	
• First flight	1952
• Cost of one plane	$53.4 million
• Maximum speed	650 mph (1,047 kph)

The Boeing *B-52 Stratofortress*—a long-range jet-powered strategic bomber—started flying for the US Air Force in 1955.

NANO

Cheapest car in the global market

- First produced | 2009
- Cost | from $2,800
- Maximum speed | 65 mph (105 kph)

Like the *Model T* Ford, the *Nano* from Tata Motors, India, offers car ownership to people who could not have otherwise afforded a car.

MALLARD

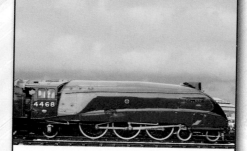

Fastest steam locomotive

- First produced | 1938
- Maximum weight | 115.3 tons
- Maximum speed | 126 mph (203 kph)

This ran on the London and North East Railway (LNER) line for 25 years, covering more than 1.5 million miles (2.4 million km).

MTT TURBINE SUPERBIKE

Most expensive motorcycle

- First produced | 2000
- Cost | $175,000
- Maximum speed | 227 mph (370 kph)

The turbojet-powered MTT Superbike is also recognized as the most powerful production motorcycle in the world.

TRIESTE

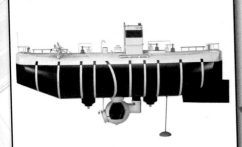

Deepest dive by a submersible

- Year of record-breaking dive | 1960
- Depth of dive | 34,797 ft (10,911 m)
- Total weight | 14.5 tons

The *Trieste* descended to the bottom of Mariana Trench in the Pacific Ocean—the deepest point in all the world's oceans.

ALLURE OF THE SEAS

Largest passenger cruise ship

- Launched in | 2010
- Total length | 1,180 ft (360 m)
- Maximum speed | 26 mph (42 kph)

Royal Caribbean International's *Allure of the Seas* can carry 6,300 passengers. It shares the size record with *Oasis of the Seas*.

ANTONOV AN-225

Heaviest cargo plane

- Year of production | 1988
- Total weight | 705 tons
- Maximum cargo capacity | 275 tons

This also holds the record for carrying the single heaviest cargo item—weighing 208 tons—ever transported by a plane.

SIKORSKY S-64F SKYCRANE

Largest civilian helicopter

- First used | 1962
- Total length | 70 ft (21.4 m)
- Maximum power | 4,500 horsepower

The *Sikorsky S-64F Skycrane* is a twin-turbofan heavy-lift helicopter used as an aerial crane and emergency response vehicle.

LUNAR ROVING VEHICLE

First manned vehicle on the Moon

- First used | 1971
- Cost | $213 million
- Maximum range | 22.3 miles (35.9 km)

The electrically powered Lunar Roving Vehicle (LRV), or moon buggy, first explored the Moon's surface in the *Apollo 15* mission.

VOYAGER I

Most distant vehicle from Earth

- Launched | 1977
- Distance | 10 billion miles (16 billion km)
- Total height | 12½ ft (3.8 m)

In 2010, this probe reached the edge of the solar system, but was still in radio contact with Earth.

Glossary

Fuselage

Top wing

Model of a biplane

ABS
Short for antilock braking system, ABS is an electronic control system that applies the brakes of a car smoothly to prevent skidding.

ADZE
An axlike tool used by ancient shipbuilders.

AERODYNAMICS
The science that studies the way air flows and how it interacts with objects moving through it.

ALLOY
A mixture of two or more metals (and sometimes nonmetals).

ASSEMBLY LINE
A manufacturing process in which a vehicle is assembled by workers and equipment arranged in a line to complete a set series of tasks, ending with a finished vehicle.

BIPLANE
An early type of fixed-wing aircraft with two wings, one above the other. One of the wings is often divided in two by the fuselage.

CARGO
The load carried by an aircraft, ship, truck, or other vehicle.

CARRACK
A merchant ship with multiple sails that was used by European countries between the 14th and 17th centuries.

CHASSIS
The supporting frame of a vehicle such as an automobile.

COWCATCHER
A triangular metal frame or grill at the front of a locomotive, designed to clear obstructions, such as cattle, from the rail track.

CRANKSHAFT
An axle inside an engine that converts the up-and-down movement of the pistons into the rotation of wheels or a propeller.

CURRENT
The flow of electricity through an object.

CYCLIC CONTROL
A control stick that a pilot pushes to make a helicopter fly forward.

CYLINDER
A strong metal tube inside an engine in which steam expands or a fuel ignites to push pistons up and down for the generation of power.

DENSITY
The mass of an object in relation to its size. Dense substances are heavy for their size.

DIESEL ENGINE
A type of internal combustion engine that runs on diesel fuel and uses the heat of compression instead of a spark plug to ignite the fuel.

DOWNFORCE
A stabilizing aerodynamic force pushing down on a vehicle due to the shape of the vehicle.

DRAG
The force that resists the movement of an object through air or water, slowing it down. The faster an object moves, the greater the drag.

EFFICIENCY
A measure of the amount of energy put into a machine that is transformed into useful work. For example, an energy-efficient light bulb converts more electrical energy into light than a conventional light bulb.

ELECTROMAGNET
An object, such as a metal wire coil, which behaves as a magnet when electricity flows through it.

ENVELOPE
The part of an airship or balloon that contains the gas providing the lift force.

FLUID
A substance, such as a liquid or gas, in which the atoms move freely. It has no fixed shape and flows easily.

FLYING BOAT
An aircraft with a watertight fuselage similar to a ship's hull. This allows the aircraft to move on water.

FRICTION
The force that resists the movement of two objects relative to each other, such as an airplane and the surrounding air.

FUEL CELL
A power source that generates electricity when a fuel, such as hydrogen, reacts with oxygen in air.

FULCRUM
The pivot point around which a lever turns.

FUSELAGE
The main body of an aircraft. The word comes from the French word *fuseler*, meaning "to shape like a spindle."

Robotic assembly line

Wing

Ultralight

Trike

GEAR
A wheel with "teeth" around the outside that intermesh with another toothed wheel. Gears change how the speed of a driving mechanism, such as the engine of a car, converts into the speed of the driven parts, such as its wheels.

GPS
Short for Global Positioning System, GPS is a navigational aid used to determine a user's location on Earth by comparing radio signals from each of a group of satellites.

HAWSER
Thick, metal cable or rope used by tugboats to tow larger ships, such as oil tankers, into port.

HORSEPOWER
An informal unit of power equal to the pulling power of one horse, or around 750 watts.

Radar screen

HYBRID CAR
A car that runs on two or more forms of fuel.

IMPELLER
A rotating part of a machine that increases the pressure and flow of a fluid.

INTERNAL COMBUSTION
The process of burning fuel with air inside a cylinder to generate power.

JET ENGINE
An engine that burns fuel in air to create a stream of hot exhaust gases that produces thrust in the opposite direction from the vehicle's movement.

JET SKI
A small personal watercraft, powered by jet propulsion that skims along the surface of the water.

LEVER
A simple machine that magnifies or reduces forces, making it easier to move a load. An oar is an example of a lever.

MAGNETIC FIELD
The space around a magnet within which it attracts magnetic substances and repels and attracts other magnets.

ORBIT
The motion of an object, such as a satellite, around another object, such as a planet.

OUTRIGGER
A float or extra hull set apart from the main hull that helps stabilize a boat in the water.

PANTOGRAPH
A spring-loaded frame that passes electricity to vehicles, such as trains and trolley buses, from overhead power lines.

PETROLEUM
Also known as crude oil, a liquid mixture of complex carbon-based chemicals formed from remains of long-dead living organisms. Found underground, it is extracted and refined to produce fuels for vehicles.

RADAR
Short for Radio Detection and Ranging, radar is a method of sending out pulses of radio waves that reflect off objects and return to the source. It can be used to calculate the direction, distance, and speed of aircraft, ships, and other moving objects.

RECONNAISSANCE
Military observation aimed at learning the location, activities, and resources of an enemy.

PISTON
A tightly fitting plunger that moves up and down inside a cylinder due to the pressure of steam or as fuel burns within an internal combustion engine.

PROPELLER
A set of rotating blades, powered by an engine, that drives a vehicle forward and upward.

SATELLITE
An artificial object placed in orbit around Earth or another planet or moon to collect or relay data. It also refers to natural objects such as the moons that orbit planets.

SOLAR PANEL
An assembly of solar cells that absorb the energy from sunlight to generate electricity.

STEALTH TECHNOLOGY
Designing the shape and materials of military vehicles, such as aircraft, missiles, ships, and submarines so that they are less visible by radar and other methods of detection.

SUBMERSIBLE
An underwater vessel used for scientific research or exploration or salvage work.

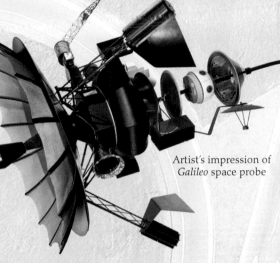

Artist's impression of *Galileo* space probe

SPACE PROBE
An unmanned instrument sent into space to collect data about heavenly bodies or space and relay the information back to Earth.

SUPERSONIC
Having a speed greater than that of sound, which is about 783 mph (1,260 kph) in air at sea level at a temperature of 68°F (20°C).

SUSPENSION
The system of springs and shock absorbers on a vehicle that smooth out bumps in the road during a ride.

THRUST
The force produced by an engine that moves a vehicle forward.

TREAD
The raised patterns on a tire's surface that increase friction between the wheels of a vehicle and the ground.

TURBINE
A machine that produces power with a rotor that spins in a fast-moving jet of air, water, or other fluid.

ULTRALIGHT
A lightweight, slow-moving aircraft in which the pilot sits in an open fiberglass car called a trike. Ultralights are also called microlights.

V-shaped tread on tire

Index

Acknowledgments

Dorling Kindersley would like to thank: Miranda Smith for proofreading; Jackie Brind for the index; Akanksha Gupta and Honlung Zach Ragui for design assistance; and Nidhi Sharma, Pallavi Singh and Bharti Bedi for editorial assistance.

The publisher would like to thank the following for their kind permission to reproduce their photographs:

(Key: a-above; b-below/bottom; c-centre; f-far; l-left; r-right; t-top)

© Airbus S.A.S. 2011: 62cl; **Alamy Images:** Alvey & Towers Picture Library 53tr, Hans Dieter Seufert / culture-images GmbH 54-55, Dario Facca 17fcr, Peter Horree 4br, 15tr, Interfoto 26cl, Lenscap 2-3tc, 56tr, Lordprice Collection 33br, Anton Luhr / Imagebroker 56-57bc, Dirk v. Mallinckrodt 23cr, Mary Evans Picture Library 36c, Motoring Picture Library 4cra, 33c, Graham Mulrooney 22cl, National Motor Museum / Motoring Picture Library 30cr, 30-31b, Forget Patrick / SAGAPHOTO.COM 57tr, PCN Black / PCN Photography 31c, Fluger Rene / CTK 54cr, Rainer Unkel / vario images 25tr, Washington Stock Photo 51c, World History Archive 30bl; **Australian National Maritime Museum:** Spirit of Australia is part of the museum's collection 66tr; **The Bridgeman Art Library:** Ashmolean Museum, University of Oxford, UK 11tl, Vinci, Leonardo da / Private Collection 36cla, Private Collection 17c, Private Collection / Tarker 24b; **Bryan & Cherry Alexander / ArcticPhoto:** 8-9l; **Corbis:** Yann Arthus-Bertrand / Terra 48-49, Gaetan Bally / Keystone / Corbis Wire 53tl, David Bathgate 7tr, Oliver Berg / dpa 2cr, 36cb, Bettmann 22-25, 25br, 32tr, 43tr, Stefano Bianchetti / Historical 27tr, Michael Cole 40tc, Dean Conger 68br, Construction Photography / Terra 49cr, Gary Coronado / ZUMA Press 61cr, Richard Cummins / Encyclopedia 50-51, Gianni Dagli Orti / The Picture

Desk Limited 2tr, 11cl, Ed Darack / Science Faction / Encyclopedia 58cl, 59cra, DoD / Encyclopedia 59tl, 59cr, Thomas Frey / dpa / News Archive 69cr, Jose Fuste Raga / Terra 9br, Albert Gea / Reuters 55t, Richard Hamilton Smith / Documentary Value 65tr, Lindsay Hebberd / Terra 14-15b, Baldwin H. Ward & Kathryn C. Ward / Historical 42bc, Historical 67tr, Hulton-Deutsch Collection / Historical 25tl, Bill Ingalls / NASA / Handout / CNP 46tl, Douglas Keister 7c, moodboard 56cl, Museum of Flight / Historical 34-35, Bill Nation / Sygma 67bl, David Pollack / K.J. Historical 25c, Reuters 11br, Reuters / Tata / Handout 69tl, Paul Russell / Comet 51cr, Rykoff Collection 65bl, Michele Sandberg / Zuma Press 69c, Smithsonian Institution 64br, Joseph Sohm / Visions of America / Encyclopedia 65cl, Guy Spangenberg / TRANSSTOCK / Transstock / Encyclopedia 69bl, Stapleton Collection / Historical Picture Library 13tl, Swim Ink 2, LLC 33br, Swim Ink 2, LLC / Fine Art 48cl, Terra 42-43t; Topic Photo Agency / Documentary 13br, Tim Wright / Terra 60cl, Niu Yixin / XinHua / Xinhua Press / Corbis Wire 52-53b; **Dorling Kindersley:** National Motor Museum, Beaulieu 3c, 4cla, 32cla, 32cl, 32fcla, 32-33, 33cla, 33ca, 41c, 2clb, 31t, 64cl, Exeter Maritime Museum 4tl, 10bl,10l,11tr National Maritime Museum, London 10r, 16tl, 16cl, The Trustees of the British Museum 11b, Museum of London 15bc, Courtesy Mercedes-Benz Cars, Daimler AG 41cl, Keith Atkinson 57cl, BMW Sauber F1 Team 4bl, 54tl, Garry Darby / American 50's Car Hire 41t, National Railway Museum, York 18-19b, 21cr, 69tc, Patrick Racing, CART, 2001 71br, Science Museum, London 4cl, 12bc, 12br, 13tr, 18tl, 19tl, 38cl, 69cl; **Dreamstime.com:** Sculpies 5tr, 49t, Gordon Tipene 2-3b, 50-51t; **ESA:** D. Ducros 42-43c; **Getty Images:** Slim Aarons / Premium Archive 61br, AFP / DDP 68c, Apic / Hulton Archive 34cl, 40-41, H. Armstrong Roberts / Retrofile 40c, Blank Archives / Hulton Archive 25bl, Thierry Boccon-Gibod 62-63tc, Bride Lane Library / Popperfoto 48tr, Tony Cordoza /

Photographer's Choice RF 55br, Antonio Giovanni de Varese / The Bridgeman Art Library 64tr, Adrian Dennis / AFP 39b, Sue Flood / Photographer's Choice 6tr, Sean Gallup 65cr, Pete Gardner / Photodisc 53cl, Tom Grill / Iconica 21tr, Tim Hales / Stringer 68bc, Handout / Getty Images News 46-47t, Charles Hewitt / Hulton Archive 39tl, Hulton Archive 35cl, Imagno / Hulton Archive 27b, 28tl, Kurita Kaku / Gamma-Rapho 52tl, Keystone-France / Gamma-Keystone 35br, Junko Kimura 55cl, Dan Kitwood 8bc, Mario Laporta / AFP 7br, Macedonian School / The Bridgeman Art Library 9c, Clive Mason 68tr, David Paul Morris 37cra, Francois Nascimbeni / AFP 66b, Scott Nelson 58b, Jeffrey Phelps 57tl, 70-71c, Joern Pollex 68cl, Popperfoto 33cr, Cristina Quicler / AFP 39tr, Joe Raedle 65br, Last Refuge / Robert Harding World Imagery 14tr, Rischgitz / Hulton Archive 9bl, Science & Society Picture Library 1tr, 12tl, 19tr, 20tl, 29c, 35tr, 65tl, Check Six 38tr, Slobo / The Agency Collection 64-65, 66-67, 68-69, SuperStock 6-7c, Topical Press Agency / Stringer / Hulton Archive 68bl, Yoshikatsu Tsuno / AFP 55cr, Toru Yamanaka / AFP 51br; Used with permission, GM Media Archives: 62b; **MTT – Leading Turbine Innovation:** www.marineturbine.com 69tr; **NASA:** JPL 46-47b, JPL-Caltech 69br, Kennedy Space Center 44-45c, Lockheed Martin Corp. 47c, NASA Great Images in Nasa Collection 69bc, NASA Great Images 47tr, Project Apollo Archive 45cra, 45cr, Saturn Apollo Program 4tr, 45bc; **NAVY.mil:** Adam K. Thomas 60-61c, 61tr, Lt. Cmdr. Eric Tidwell 58-59; **OpenFlights.org:** http://opendatacommons.org/ licenses / odbl / 1.0 49cl; **Panos Pictures:** Georg Gerster 22bl; **Photolibrary:** Bob Burch / Index Stock Imagery 26-27c, Claver Carroll / Ticket 16-17c, 21cla, Images of Birmingha / Loop Images 70b, Carol Kohen / Cultura RM 49bc, Movementway Movementway / Imagebroker.net 21br, Worldscapes Worldscapes / Age fotostock 20-21b; **Mark Von Raesfeld:** 36-37t; Science Museum / Science &

Society Picture Library: National Railway Museum 23tc, NRM Pictorial Collection 19cr; **Science Photo Library:** Walter Myers 63br; **SuperStock:** Science and Society 65tc, The Francis Frith Collection 40cl; **TopFoto.co.uk:** Topham Picturepoint 23br, ullsteinbild 30c; **ULTra PRT** - www.ultraprt.com: 62cr

Jacket images: Front: Corbis: Theo Allofs b; **Dorling Kindersley:** National Motor Museum, Beaulieu tc; *Back:* **Alamy Images:** Interfoto cr, National Motor Museum / Motoring Picture Library br; **Corbis:** Creasource tr, Araldo de Luca cl; **Dorling Kindersley:** A.J. Pozner (Hendon Way Motors) bl; **Getty Images:** Stan Honda / AFP cra

Wallchart: Airbus S.A.S. 2011: Airbus SAS 2011 fbr; **Alamy Images:** Hans Dieter Seufert / culture-images GmbH ca; **Dorling Kindersley:** Exeter Maritime Museum cla, National Railway Museum, York cb, The Science Museum, London cl; **Getty Images:** Imagno / Hulton Archive br; **NASA:** Kennedy Space Center br; **NAVY.mil:** Lt. Cmdr. Eric Tidwell crb; **Photolibrary:** Claver Carroll / Ticket bl, Worldscapes Worldscapes / Age fotostock c

All other images © Dorling Kindersley
For further information see: www.dkimages.com

J
388
Gra

Transportation.
TOT
33900903212878
$12.39